JUST SAY THANK YOU

JUST SAY THANK YOU

♦

A REAL LIFE STORY OF A NEW YORK CITY EMERGENCY MEDICAL TECHNICIAN

James Thompson

iUniverse, Inc.

New York Lincoln Shanghai

JUST SAY THANK YOU
A REAL LIFE STORY OF A NEW YORK CITY EMERGENCY MEDICAL TECHNICIAN

iUniverse books may be ordered through booksellers or by contacting:

iUniverse
2021 Pine Lake Road, Suite 100
Lincoln, NE 68512
www.iuniverse.com
1-800-Authors (1-800-288-4677)

ISBN-13: 978-0-595-37519-6 (pbk)
ISBN-13: 978-0-595-81912-6 (ebk)
ISBN-10: 0-595-37519-7 (pbk)
ISBN-10: 0-595-81912-5 (ebk)

Printed in the United States of America

THIS BOOK IS DEDICATED TO ALL THE
EMERGENCY MEDICAL TECHNICIANS
AND PARAMEDICS.

SPECIAL DEDICATION TO ALL THOSE
THAT HAVE MADE THE SUPREME
SACRAFICE IN THE PERFORMANCE
OF THEIR JOB.

SPECIAL THANKS TO IRENE THOMPSON, DAN
MULLINS, STEVEN JEROME AND DORIS KESSLER
FOR THEIR ASSISTANCE IN THIS BOOK.

Contents

<u>ABOUT THIS BOOK</u>

This book is about the real life of a New York City Emergency Medical Technician. It will take you through the good times and the bad times. I hope you enjoy this book.

THE ASSIGNMENT

It is about 7 PM. The radio blares, "45 David for the assignment you have a sick call on the corner of Metropolitan and 53 St."

"45 David ten four".

My partner Bob starts to write down the assignment on the back of the ambulance Call report. I am driving and start to turn on the lights and siren. Bob presses MR into the computer on the bus. This command will bring up all the information on the call. It states that there is a female on the corner with a headache and wants to go to the hospital. We think this is a real emergency. Why does she not take a cab to the hospital? In New York, the people treat EMS as their own taxi service, and you learn to live with it.

We are heading down Tonsor Street, when two police cars pass use lights and sirens on.

Bob states, "They must have something good".

The next thing we hear is "45 David for the higher priority"

I pick up the mike, "45 David Queens",

"Queens 45 David responds to the gun shot on Peteman Street. Report of a person shot five times."

I reply "45 David ten-four."

We make a U turn in the middle of the street and head to the new job.

I say "Oh well, the headache can wait. We have a real job"

Bob pulls up the MR on the computer. He starts reading it out loud to me over the sound of the siren. I am driving fast with the siren and lights on. I turn on to Myrtle Avenue. Traffic is pretty clear. People are moving to the side of the street, so we can get through. That is unusual in New York for people to move out of the way of an emergency vehicle.

I make the left turn onto Fresh Ponds Road. Traffic is starting to get heavier. I then made a left onto Peteman Street. There is a big city bus in the way. The police are yelling over the radio, "Put a rush on the bus" that is what they call an ambulance in the city of New York. The bus finally moves. We pull-up between a couple of parked cars.

There is a body of a young man lying on the ground face down. He has been shot once to the head. "45 David Queens need medics. One shot to the head".

"45 David you have 46 Willie responding. They should be there soon."

"Ten-four."

About this time I hear 46 Willie sirens. They are an excellent medic crew to work with. Bob takes the oxygen and tech bag to check the patient. I get the long board, c-collar, and stretcher out of the bus. We roll the patient onto the long board and put him on the stretcher. There is a large crowd and numerous police officers on the scene. People are asking use "Is he alive?"

We place him in the back of the ambulance. Bob starts to clear his airway using a suction unit. I can hear the gurgle sound it makes clearing his airway. I pull all his clothes off. There is a detective in the ambulance with use now. I hand him all the patient's clothes. 46 Willie arrives on the scene. They grab their medic equipment and get in the back of our bus. They tell me to get into the driver seat, and get ready to head to the closest hospital.

I grab the mike, "45 David Queens with a priority".

"45 David go ahead"

"Notify hospital. 58 enroute with a 28 year old male. One shot to the head, no exit wound. CPR in progress 46 Willie with use. ETA about six minutes".

"Queens ten-four"

We start heading toward the hospital. I have my lights and sirens on. The police are in front of me with their lights and sirens on. We get to the hospital in about six minutes. I back the ambulance into the loading dock. I get up and jump onto the loading dock area, and open the back doors. There are the medics working on the patient. They have intubated the patient, started intravenous lines, and have him hooked up to the heart monitor. He does not look good. The monitor is only showing activity when compressions are being done. I am careful not to move the tube or disconnect the intravenous lines or monitor. We pull the stretcher out and take him into the emergency room. Bob jumps up on the side rail of the stretcher. He is performing CPR on the patient. I am at the head of the patient. I am squeezing the bag that is delivering oxygen to him. We carefully move him into the emergency room. They are waiting for use. We place him on the emergency room stretcher. The medics give the doctors the patient's report. I go back out and start to clean the back of the ambulance. It has blood and used equipment all over the back. It will take me a good forty-five minutes to clean it up.

I call Queens to tell them to "Put me out BBP" (Blood Born Pathogens). Bob comes out and tells me the patient did not make it. I reply "Oh well" I finishing cleaning up the back of the ambulance. We are now backs in service to get the next job. Bob presses the 97 button on the computer. This tells the dispatcher that we are in our area and ready for another job. We head back to our area. There is not much to say. We get in our area and press the 89 button on the computer. This tells the dispatcher we are at our cross street location.

It has been a couple of days since the shooting. Nothing much has happened to talk about. There has just been the regular old bullshit. Calls like, "I have a headache, take me to the hospital."

It is an hour into our shift. All of the sudden the radio blares "45 David for the adult asthma no ALS available". "45 David ten-four". I am teching today.

I go "Oh shit an asthma job"

Bob knows where we are going. He knows Queens real well. I pull out the new protocol for asthma attacks. We are now allowed to administer the drug Alburteol to patients. I need to read the protocol on the back of the Ambulance Call Report. It has a scale and other information we need to know.

We pull up in front of the address. There is an elderly lady outside waving to us. She tells us that her daughter is in side having an asthma attack please hurry. We go inside. There is a lady in her late twenties wheezing. She states that this has been going on for two days.

I ask her "Why did you not go to the hospital sooner?"

She replied "I do not like hospitals".

I pulled out the Ambulance Call Report and started to follow the instructions on the back. Bob takes her vital signs and listens to her lungs. They are tight and wheezing. I put the nebulizer together and place the drug Alburteol in it. The patient knows what to do with it. I ask her all the important questions. She states to me that she has severe asthma. We carry her to the ambulance in the stair chair. She finishes the first treatment. I listen to her lungs. They are still wheezing, so I give her a second treatment. She states that the second treatment is starting to help her breath easier.

I tell Bob to notify the hospital that we have an asthma job. He tells "Queens 45 David for the notification hospital 32, 28 female asthma two treatments ETA six minutes"

"45 David ten-four hospital notified"

By time we arrive we arrive at the hospital she is doing fine. We give the report to the triage nurse, and turn her over to the emergency room staff. There is another ambulance crew at the hospital. They are asking us about the shooting the other night. So, we tell them all about it. You can only stay at the hospital for about twenty minutes. After that the dispatcher starts calling you for up dates. Then they will send a patrol supervisor to the hospital to check up on you. We get done talking to the crew and go 97 on the computer.

We had back to the station to replace the equipment. It takes about fifteen minutes to get there. We talk about that last job. How we are doing more work? And the city is not paying use any more money for it. We get to the station.

"You have to sign for the Alburteol, The captain has a fit if the count is off" states Lieutenant Cape.

Lieutenant Cape gives us the drugs and makes use sign for them.

He asks us "How did the asthma job go?"

We reply "Never fear 45 David is here"

He laughs and tells us to get out and do our job. We get back in our bus and leave the station. All the sudden we get a message from Queens dispatch.

We are to go to the 204 Police Precinct station. That the detectives want to talk to use about the shooting the other day. We start to head over to the police station. It will take us about ten minutes to get there. Bob and I are talking about the job. We arrive at the station and head up stairs to the detective's squad office. The detective comes out.

He states "I have questions for you guys in reference to the shooting the other day"

"OK what do you want to now"?

"Did the patient say anything"?

"No he was in traumatic arrest" I reply

"Did anybody say anything to you at the scene"?

"No", I reply

He states "This is my first murder investigation. Is there anything else I need to know"? I said "No"

He then proceeded to tell us what happened.

He tells us 'This guy went over to see his child, and his girlfriend's new boy-friend shot him.

I state 'That sucks"

We talk a little longer about the job. He asks us about the fire department emergency medical service merger. We tell him what we think about it and how it is working out. We then head back to the bus. He tells us that there is a warrant out for the boyfriend. He then thanks us for coming by the station.

THE ACADEMY

A friend and I were talking one day down in Maryland. We were talking about working for New York City since they are the busiest in the nation. We decided if we were going to do emergency medical service for a career, we might as well work for the busiest city in the nation. We talked about it for a couple of days. We always saw pictures of New York City in magazines. They always show the fire department and emergency medical services working on the good jobs. Not what we have down here in Maryland. So this looked like it would be a challenging job. If there were anything we would have wanted, it would be a challenge. So we decided to drive up and apply for a job with New York City Emergency Medical Service. I had a cousin that lived in the Throngsneck section of the Bronx. We called her and she said that we could stay there for the night. I forgot to get the directions to her house.

We then decided to drive up there on a Thursday and stay there to Saturday. It was a cool fall day when we left Bethesda, Maryland. As we were loading up the truck, the talk was about New York City what we were going to do. What fire stations we would stop by visit. John wanted to check out Rescue One in Manhattan. As we left Bethesda, Maryland John was driving and I was reading the map. We headed up Interstate 95 north toward New York.

"Hey lets stop by and see my girlfriend at the University of Delaware" John said.

"OK" I reply.

"I now a way we can avoid all the tolls"

"Hey that is great" I replied.

So we headed to the University of Delaware. We met up with John's girlfriend and her roommate. We talked for a while telling them what we were going to do.

They told us to be careful. We finished our pizza and headed north toward New York City.

We were near the George Washington Bridge when John asked,

"Do you have the directions to their house"?

"Oh shit the directions are in Maryland. I have her phone number" I reply.

We called her. She gave us the directions to her house. It did not sound that hard to find her house. It was right off the expressway.

We got to where Interstate 95 divides in the Bronx.

"Which way now"? John asks.

"Oh shit, I don't know"

Well we guessed the right way. Now we were lost in the Bronx. I looked up. It is about 10 PM and I see the sign Hollywood Avenue.

"Follow Hollywood Avenue it will take use to her address. She lives in the seven hundred block." I said

We got there about 1015 that night. It was an interesting trip up to New York so far.

The next morning we got up. My cousin Vicky gave us directions to Washington Street in Manhattan where the application section was. She told us which subways to take. First we took the train to downtown Manhattan. We were going to apply for the upcoming firefighter test. It was different riding the New York City Subway system for the first time. There were people all over the place. It was standing room only. We finally got to the personal office.

We got off the train at the correct stop. We went up stairs to the street level. There were high-rise buildings all over the place. We saw the street sign that said Washington Street.

"There it is, all we have to do is follow it to the address" I said

Well, first we went the wrong way. We figured that out when the address were going up instead of down. We finally get to the application section. There is a long line of people waiting. First we went over and read the bulletin board with all the job announcements on it. Then we went to the window with the line. There was a lady behind the glass window. We told her we wanted the applications for firefighter. She gave us the applications.

We filled out the applications and went to the Post Office for a twenty-five dollar money order. It was a very simple application to fill out. Just name, address, phone number, and date of birth. After we filled out the application we drop them in the mail.

"Hey John lets go to the World Trade Center, I want to apply for the airport fire department with the Port Authority"

"OK lets go" he replies.

We head over to the World Trade center. We get there and it is these two big square boxes. I feel dizzy just looking up at them. We head up to the forty-fourth floor, where the application section is.

We enter the application section. There is a lady there.

"May I help you"?

"Yes I want to apply for firefighter at the airports"

"I am sorry but you have to be a police officer first".

"I do not want to be a police officer all I want to be is a firefighter"

Then she explains to me that you have to be both a police officer and a firefighter. They are not excepting applications at this time. She gives us a number to call to see when they will be excepting applications. We thank here and then decide to go to the top of the towers.

We head back out to the elevator bank. You have to take a couple of elevators to get to the top. We finally get to the top, and take the stairs to the observation deck. You can feel the change in temperature and the wind blowing in my hair. It is really nice you can see parts on New Jersey, Connecticut, and all of New York City.

"Hey John look, that is where we are staying in the Bronx"

"Yea this is cool" he replies.

We do the tourist thing take a couple of pictures. We have been up here for about thirty minutes when we decide to leave. We take the express elevator down to the ground. You can feel your ears pop as you descend to the lobby. I think it was a nice experience.

From there, we decided to go apply for New York City Emergency Medical Service. We saw a firestation. It was Engine Ten and Ladder Ten or the Ten House as it is know. They told us that New York City Emergency Medical Service was located in the borough of Queens. They told us there was an EMS station near South Street Seaport. They then told us how to get there. We walked to the station. It took us about thirty minutes. All the time we were talking about working for the city. It was Station Eleven. We went inside. There was a lieutenant sitting at the desk.

"Excuse me sir we are from Bethesda, Maryland and want to apply for a job with the New York City Emergency Medical Service" I said.

"You have to go to Maspeth Queens for the application process" he replied.

"Where is that"?

He told us which subways to take to get there. We were off again for a trip on the subways again.

We were asking police officers on the subways how to get to Queens. One officer told us he worked for EMS. He gave us directions to their headquarters. That helped us a lot. You could tell we did not live in the city of New York. We were always asking directions all the time.

We finally got to Queens. Now all we had to do is get to 58th Street and 47th Avenue in Maspeth Queens. We got on the correct bus at the subway station. We told the bus driver that we were looking for EMS headquarters. He told us we were on the right bus and he would drop us off there.

I said, "That would be great, Thanks a lot"

The bus driver was telling us about his volunteer experience on Long Island. It made the bus ride interesting. There were only three of us on the bus at this time. He dropped us off at the EMS headquarters.

We went in to the building and were told "You are in the wrong building. You have to go to this building down the street. Here are the directions."

I replied "Thanks a lot, see you."

We opened the door and went into the office. There was a lady there and EMT Lopez "Can I help you"?

"Yes we want to apply for New York City Emergency Medical Service," I said.

I thought he was a chief since he was wearing a white shirt. He gave us the applications and told us we had to fill them out here.

He then said, "I need a copy of your New York State driver's license and EMT card".

I said, "We are from Maryland. Can we take the applications with us"?

"Hold on I will check" he replied

"Yes you can, but you have to get a New York state EMT card to apply" he said.

I said "OK and mail it back"

Well we mailed the application back using certified mail. Six months went by I did not hear anything. I would call up there and ask what the status of my application was.

"They would always reply, "We have it on file. We will be calling you soon."

Well it was about a year and a half when they called.

Then one night in May I was working at my volunteer station in Bethesda Maryland. The phone rings. The person asks for me. It was Vicky.

She says, "James you have been hired by New York City Emergency Medical Service, and you start June 4 1994"

I reply "Great"

I start thinking to my self, what is in store for me. So the end of May I move to New York.

I drove up to New York thinking about the job, and what all I will be doing. The first thing I needed to do was a find place to live. So I got a large map of the area. One of the city and one for Nassau County. I did not want to live far from the academy. My first day in New York I started to search for an apartment. I saw on the map, the City of Long Beach. It was on the ocean, and I like the beach. I though of hanging out on the beach during the day, and going to the clubs at nighttime. During the summer there would be women all over the place. I was right. I found a small studio apartment one block from the beach.

It was my first day in the academy. I pull out my map I find my way to the academy. I leave early to give my self-time in case I get lost. It was not as hard as I was thought it would be to get to the academy. I find the building and the room with all the new students. There are thirty-five of us in the class. In walks this tall Lieutenant. You can tell he is strictly business. He tells us his name is Lieutenant Tom and he is our officer in charge. He calls out everybody's name, and tells us about the academy.

He tells us "That we must maintain at least a seventy-five percent or we will be terminated."

I think I have been an Emergency Medical Technician for a long time. I should not have trouble passing these tests. He finishes his lecture by telling us that half of us will not make it, and that a third of us will fail in the first two weeks.

Then two other men come in the room. They tell us their names. They are Jim Man and Mike Dave. They are Instructor Coordinators for our class. They tell us that we will be given a test everyday, with a final at the end of each week. They tell us that are scores will be posted by social security number on the wall after lunch at the door after lunch. After lunch we are handed numerous forms to fill out and receive all our books.

It is now the second day in class. We go in, have a seat and roll is taken. Then we are handed our test. It is a one hundred questions. I read the questions. These are not the simple questions. These are the type questions you get asked when becoming an Emergency Medical Technician for the first time. I know I need to study if I am going to pass. Then we get our morning lecture. It is after lunch now. We come in and everybody checks the list. I see that I have passed. There are a couple of numbers highlighted. They report to the Lieutenant's office. They are told they will have to bring their score up or they will be fired.

Well it is the fourth day of class. Instructor Man is lecturing us.

I ask, "Say Instructor Man since the firefighters are on the scene can they drive the ambulance to the hospital since we have a bad patient"?

Instructor Man looks at me and says, "Where do you think you are California"?

I say, "No I am in New York now I was there last week"

"You do not let them touch your equipment or vehicle" he replies.

I reply "OK"

He goes on about letting firefighters drive our vehicles. At this point the whole class starts chanting, "He is going back to California" that has become my nickname.

Well it is the end of the week. We are getting ready to take our first final. We have lost six students in the class. For not maintaining the seventy-five percent. They pass out the test. It is as hard as the quiz you get everyday. I take the test and wonder if I passed. After lunch, I check my score. And yes, I did pass. The next part of training will be the Operations Guide. This is called the New York City Emergency Medical Service bible. We will spend a week learning the guide.

They tell us to go to the downstairs supply room. We head down the stairs to the basement. We line up and a guy hands us these big heavy notebook binders. It says on the cover Emergency Medical Services City of New York Operations Guide. This book is about four inches thick.

"OK people for the next week. We are going to learn the operations guide. This is the EMS bible. It is not as hard as it looks" Jim tells us.

We head back up to the classroom. The book is heavy and cumbersome. We start looking through it. When another instructor comes in the room.

"My name is Instructor Kenny Berry. You people can call me Ken. OK lets take a fifteen minute break" he tells us.

We come back in to the room.

"As you can see this book covers everything you need to now to do the job. It is thick but a lot of it is common sense" he tells us.

I page through the book when I get home from class. It covers everything. But it does not appear that hard to understand. And of course we will be tested on it everyday till we graduate from the academy. We are now about four weeks in to training. We have two weeks of operations guide training. This is to make sure we now what we are doing.

We have finished the operations guide part of our training. We have only lost six people. We are at the halfway point in the academy.

It is now July in New York and it is hot and humid in the afternoon. We are getting ready to go to the Emergency Vehicle Operators Course. Lieutenant Mitchell teaches it. He comes in to the class.

"Lieutenant Mitchell states to us "You will be on an airfield. It gets hot bring water with you".

We start our training in the mourning it is nice and cool. There is a nice breeze blowing off the ocean. But in the afternoon it gets hot and humid. We break for lunch.

Lieutenant Mitchell tells use "It is to hot to train this afternoon".

A couple of us go to Toys-R-Us and by supersoakers. Well in the afternoon it is so hot and humid. You sweat just standing there. We start having water fights. The next thing you now everybody is wet. It feels real good. It has been two weeks we are all trained to drive the ambulances. Now it is back to the academy building for our last week of training.

It is the last week of training. All we have left is group roll play. This is where they give you one medical and one trauma scenario. You have to treat the patient the patient and transport to the proper hospital. I get my first scenario it is an allergic reaction to a bee sting. I can do this one easy because I am highly allergic to bees. I perform all the correct steps. The instructor watches me carefully. I then get my trauma scenario. It is a person that has fallen off a three-story building. I perform all the correct steps for the patient. The instructor tells me to leave the room. It is lunchtime everybody has done his or her scenario.

Lieutenant Tom comes in the room. He calls out seven names. Mine is one of the names. He tells us "You have passed the academy and to stay outside after lunch". All that is left now is graduation and that is on Tuesday.

Well Tuesday comes. Everybody is excited we are all graduating. We get issued our shields and identification cards. We are now employees of the New York City Emergency Medical Service. At the graduation we present are Instructors Coordinators Jim Man, Mike Dave and Lieutenant Tom with a plaque of apparition. We are given the next day off before reporting to the borough we are assigned to.

Today we report to the Brooklyn Borough Command. There we meet the chief and all the staff. I am reading my map so I do not get lost. I have never been in Brooklyn. I am thinking about where I am going to be assigned. Will it be a busy station in a ghetto or a slow station in a middle class or rich neighbor hood?

Lieutenant Geno comes in the room. He gives us a lot of paperwork to fill out. All the forms require your name, address, and phone number, driver's license number, and emergency medical technician number. He tells us about Brooklyn. We are all wondering where we are going to be assigned in Brooklyn. Brooklyn is the largest and busiest borough in the City of New York. It is now lunchtime. A group of us walk to McDonalds it is down the street. We are all talking about what lies ahead of us. I am not from New York so I know very little about Brooklyn. I know there are some bad areas such as Bedford Stevysant. But I just listen and try to learn as everybody in the group talks.

It is after lunch we return to the station. At this point Lieutenant Geno ask for everybody social security number. He tells use the lower the social security number. You get to pick the station you want to go to

I am hoping for Coney Island "Since that is the only station I now how to get to". My turn comes up I tell him "Coney Island Station thirty-one"

He replies "That is where you will be assigned".

I feel great I can get there without getting lost. We are told to report to the station the next mourning at 0800 hours. Well we finish up the day and I drive back to my apartment in Long Beach. On the way home I am wondering what my assignment will be like. Is Coney Island going to be a busy station? Or is it a rich area where there is very little work. I will find out tomorrow when I report.

CONEY ISLAND
MY FIRST ASSIGNMENT

It is my first day on the job. I get up early as not to be late. I look at the map and figure out the best way to the station. It is to take Rockaway Turnpike to the Belt Parkway to Coney Island hospital. The station is located behind the hospital. I have to be there by 0800 in the mourning.

I put on my uniform for which I am proud to where. There is a light ocean breeze as I leave my apartment. I stop off at the bagel store for a bagel and a liter bottle of Diet Coke. It wakes me up in the mourning. And I do not like the smell of coffee. I head toward Rockaway Turnpike. There is little traffic on the road. Which makes it easy for me to look around and get my bearings. I get on the Belt Parkway. The traffic is moving at a faster pace. Everybody is in a hurry in New York. I see the sign for Coney Island Hospital. I know it is not far now. I get to the station about 0730 hours. I am early like I planned.

I walk in to the office. There is a lieutenant sitting behind the desk.

"May I help you," he asks.

"Yes my name is James Thompson I am suppose to report here today" I reply.

"OK I will talk to you after roll call. Go have a seat in the lounge" he tells me.

"Yes sir", I reply.

"Hello my name is Lieutenant Al Sutton. I have some paperwork for you to fill out. Do you have all your equipment"?

"Yes sir".

"What tour would you like"?

"I would like to be on tour three or tour one".

He looks at the master schedule.

"OK you will be on tour three B platoon. Your start time will be fifteen hundred hours or three o'clock in the afternoon".

"Yes sir".

I fill out all the paperwork and give it to him.

"Do you have a nickname or what do you prefer to be called"?

I reply "Cali since I am from California and that is what they called me in the academy".

"You have to go see the captain and the chief now. Go through the door to the trailer that is where there office is".

"OK thank you".

I go over to the trailer and knock on the door. The captain tells me to come in.

"Hello my name is Captain Roth".

He takes my paperwork from me. He tells me that I am vacation relief on tour three B platoon. He tells me about the various policies and procedures at the station. He then introduces me to Chief Hard. He is the station chief.

"Do you have any questions" the chief asks.

"No" I reply.

"OK you report tomorrow at fifteen hundred hours see you then".

"Yes sir".

It is my first shift on the ambulance. I am driving to work wondering about what I am going to be doing. I have worked in the emergency medical service in California. There I saw and did a lot. But in New York the largest city in the nation and the busiest. Who knows I am driving down the Belt Parkway to the station with all that is going through my mind? I get to the station, park my truck and go inside. Put on my uniform and grab my tech bag and equipment. Then I sit in the lounge and wait for roll call. All the time I am meeting the personal assigned the station. They are all very nice and friendly toward me the new man in the station. Then I hear "roll call roll call" over the public address system. I report to the office.

"Good afternoon men, we have a new man assigned here, his name is James Thompson they call him Cali".

I meet everybody in the station. He then tells us what unit we will be assigned to.

"Cali you are working Thirty-One-David with Ron Smith".

"Yes sir".

"OK let's go to work and be safe out there".

We go out to the ambulance. I am technician Ron is driving. I get the checklist and start checking all the equipment on the ambulance.

Ron tells me "We are working in the pit".

That is the area down near the amusement park at Coney Island. I go get the checkout sheet signed by the lieutenant.

He states to me "You are on B platoon".

"Yes sir".

"I am you lieutenant my name is Lieutenant McNash".

I shake his hand and head out to the bus.

We head out of the station parking lot to go to our area.

"Is there anything you want to get to drink or eat"? Ron Ask.

"No thanks I am all right maybe later".

"Thirty-One-David for the sick" the dispatcher calls.

"Thirty-One-David give it up" responded Ron over the radio.

Then the computer lights up with the job information on it. Ron hits the sixty-three button. That means we are responding to the call. I pull up the MR on the call. It does not give us much information.

"Thirty-One-David eighty-seven the assignment" the dispatcher tell us.

That means disregard the call. As the night goes on we get eleven more calls. And each time that we start responding to the job we get told to disregard. Either the caller does not want an ambulance or another unit takes the call. I am starting to wonder am I ever going to see any action.

Then we get a call about ten o'clock at night.

"Thirty-One-David for the ped struck at West 18 Street and Mermaid" the dispatcher.

We acknowledge the call, and press the sixty-three button and start responding with the siren and lights on. We arrive at the scene. There is a young boy lying on the ground. His head split open. And his left leg is bent and turned in the wrong direction. It is obviously broken. He is yelling in pain. I grab my tech bag, oxygen and head to him. Ron opens the back compartment. He grabs the backboard and cervical collar and heads toward the patient.

I check his airway. It is clear. I start asking him questions. He is confused and can not answer them properly. This is a sign of a serious head injury. I dress and bandage the large wound on his head. It is still actively bleeding. Then we put a cervical collar on his neck. This is to protect his neck from any injury. We then splint his fractured leg. It is a compound fracture. You can see the bone ends sticking out through the skin. We are now ready to roll him on to the backboard.

About this time a women comes running up to the scene screaming. She tries to grab him. But the police on the scene restrain her. The police now this child is in critical condition. We tell them we are taking him to Coney Island Hospital since it is a trauma center. They will take the mother in the patrol car to the hospital.

We get the patient in the back of the bus. I get a real quick set of vital signs, pulse, respiration and blood pressure. I write them down on a piece of paper. And pass it through the window boot to Ron.

"Thirty-One-David to Brooklyn South with a notification to Hospital thirty-two".

"Go ahead Thirty-One-David with your notification".

"Thirty-One-David inbound with a one four year old male, large laceration and contusion to the head, compound fracture of left leg, hit by a car, not alert and oriented, vitals are as follows B/P 110/60 pulse 100 respiration 20 about four minutes out".

"Ten-four Thirty-One-David Emergency Room waiting for you".

We start heading toward the hospital. Our lights and sirens are on. I have the patient on high flow oxygen. This is to help keep the brain from swelling. But his respirations are starting to increase. This is not a good sign. This means the brain is starting to swell. So I get out the Ambu bag and start forcing oxygen in to him. He still has a good airway. We arrive at the hospital and wheel the child into the trauma room. I give my report to the trauma team. And we move the patient onto the trauma stretcher. It is about ten thirty at night now. I get off work at eleven o'clock. We still have to clean up the back of the bus and restock the unit. We get back in the ambulance and drive around to the station. There we will clean up and restock the ambulance. By this time it will be time to go home for the night.

Well I have survived my first day on the job. I feel good but a little tired as I take my uniform off and put my equipment away. Now all I have to do is drive home. I figure I will stop for a beer at one of the bars in Long Beach. The drive home goes a lot faster then the drive to work. There is no traffic on the road. I get home in about thirty minutes.

I am on my third day of work at Coney Island. I am driving on the Belt Parkway when the traffic starts backing up. As I get closer there are flashing lights and police cars across the roadway. The police department blocks it off. They are directing traffic off at Rockaway Parkway. I get off the next thing I now I am lost in Brooklyn. I try finding my way to the station. But I am getting deeper into Brooklyn. Brooklyn is the largest borough. I have now driving for about thirty minutes. I am starting to see the Manhattan skyline. I think to myself oh shit you are lost. And I am going to be late to the station. I call the station from a pay phone.

"Station thirty-one Lieutenant Sutton may I help you"?

"Yes sir this is Jim Thompson, I am lost in Brooklyn".

"Where are you"?

"I am not sure but I can see the Manhattan skyline".

"How did you get there"?

"They closed the Belt Parkway and forced me off at Rockaway Parkway".

"OK relax you will be late, tell me what you see".

"There is a freeway near me I278".

"OK now listen take the expressway towards the Verrazano Bridge, then take the Shore Parkway to Coney Island Hospital. You should be here in about forty-five minutes.

"OK thanks sir".

I get in my truck and start following the directions. It takes me about forty-five minutes to get to the station.

"Cali you made it".

"Yes sir".

"Hey Cali for the next couple of days you will be working with Rudy Biggs" the desk lieutenant tells me as I enter the office to sign in.

"No problem sir, who is the"?

"I will introduce you to him when he gets here".

I go into the lounge and sit down.

"Hey Cali Rudy is here".

"Yes sir".

I enter the office.

"Hi I am Rudy I guess we are working together for the next couple of days. I do not like to drive".

"No problem I do not now Brooklyn that well".

"I do" he replies.

We head out to the ambulance.

"Is there anyplace you want to go"?

"No".

"OK well I am going to stop at Seven-Eleven to get a Diet Coke".

"OK".

All of the sudden the radio calls out "Three-Zero-David for the EDP".

That is the term for an emotional disturbed person. She gives us the address it is 3710 Lake place.

"Ten-four".

"Do you need me to look it up on the map"?

"No I know about where it is at".

We start out for the job. We turn right onto Ocean Parkway. We head up the Parkway to and turn left on Avenue P.

"Hey Rudy are you shore you now where we are going"?

"Yes I think it is over that way".

We make a u turn and start heading in the opposite direction.

The dispatcher calls us "Three-Zero-David are you eighty-eight yet"?

"No we should be there in a couple of minutes".

It has now been twenty minutes into the call. We are still looking for the street.

"Hey Cali I think it is over this way".

At the next intersection I turn left.

"Rudy are you shore you now where we are going"?

"Yes do not weary about it".

"I only have a couple of days in the field and do not want to get in trouble".

"You will not get in trouble I am a union delegate".

That makes me feel a little more relaxed. The dispatcher calls us a second time. We tell her we will be there in a couple of minutes. That the traffic is heavy. We have now been responding for about thirty-five minutes. We finally see a sign that says Lake Place. We turn down the street and find the address. I press the eighty-eight button on the computer.

The police meet us at the door.

"What a busy night out there we have been waiting for you guys for about forty-five minutes".

"Yes it is real busy tonight".

"OK this is what you have".

The police officer starts telling us about that patient. He states that the patient feels depressed and wants to hurt himself. Rudy goes in and starts getting all the information and talking to the patient. I tell the cop.

"I hope you are riding with us, I do not now the area that well".

"OK we will ride with you, just follow us to the hospital".

I think to my self great. I now feel a lot more relaxed.

"Hey EMS we are going to take him to the county".

That is short for Kings County Medical Center.

"Ok how do you get there"?

"Just follow us in the police car. It is at the New York Avenue and Clarkson Street".

"OK please do go to fast. I do not want to get lost" I reply.

"OK are you ready"?

"Shore lets go".

I follow the police car. It takes use about fifteen minutes to get to the hospital. We head around to the G building. That is where the physic patients go.

I park the ambulance. Rudy and the patient get out. We all head toward the entrance of the building. You first go through the first set of sliding glass doors. Then you stop and the doors shut. Then you go through a second set of sliding glass doors. Then they go shut. I get this feeling like I am in jail. There are hospital police all over the place.

Rudy starts to give the nurse the report. She finally agrees to sign for the patient. She signs the bottom of the report. We then get ready to leave. I can not wait to get out of there. We motion to the cop at the window to open the doors. I feel a lot better now that I am outside.

"Where are we going from here"?

"Do not worry Cali I now the way back" Rudy states.

We head out of the parking lot.

"Do you now the where we are"?

"Hell no, I am lost".

"You are in Crown Heights where the riots were"

"OK how do we get back to our area"?

"I will show you the fast way. I do not want to get stuck doing jobs here".

"OK Rudy show me the way".

We start heading back to our area. We get back there in about ten minutes. I feel even better now that I am back near Coney Island. We have about three hours left to the end of the tour. The rest of the night is quite.

We head back to the station for change of tour.

"Hey Cali I guess I will be working with you for the next couple of days"

"OK no problem".

I stop off at good old Seven-Eleven and buy myself a Diet Coke. We get to the station, turn in paperwork. I then head to my locker. And get ready for the drive home.

"Hey Cali we are hanging out down at the beach, come hang out with us" yells Seth.

"What do you want me to bring"?

"Just stop off and pick up some beer".

He tells me where to meet them. I stop off pick up the beer and head to the tailgate party. I have a good time relax and then head home.

"OK you are working with Brian Ford, He came out of the same class you did" the desk officer tells me.

I think to myself I do not remember this guy in my class. It turns out he came out of the day class. I was in the evening class.

"Hi how are you doing, I am Cali your partner"

"I am Brian, what do you want to do drive or tech? I will tech I hope you now the area better then I do. I am from Staten Island." Brian replies.

I say, "Great I am from Los Angeles California. I now nothing about Brooklyn".

And we are working a tactual unit. They go all over the city. Where ever they are needed.

"Well we have a city map we kind find anything" I reply.

We start to check out the ambulance. I go log us on to the computer. Are you call sign is Three-Zero-David.

Three-Zero-David report to the office over the public address system.

"Yes sir"

"You and Brian are going to be partners on the bus preeminently. Is there a problem with that"?

"No sir" I reply.

"Yes sir" Brian replies.

"This should be interesting. Considering how much we both now about Brooklyn".

"Well we now where Coney Island Hospital is. We will bring all patients here".

"Sounds good to me".

"Are you ready to get out here and go to our area, Let me get the check out sheet signed."

"Do you now where it is"?

"They said it was close to the station".

"Cool maybe it is down in the pit".

"Sounds good to me lets head down there and go ninety-seven available".

"OK".

"Where are you from in California"?

"Los Angeles".

"Where are you from Brian"?

"Staten Island, I managed a Toys-R-Us there".

"Why did you leave California and come here"?

"I got laid off from the fire department out there. And New York City was the first place to offer me a job. So I moved back here. It is a lot different back here".

"Hey are you thirsty"?

"Yes let's go to Seven-Eleven for something to drink".

"Three-Zero-David for the assignment" the dispatcher calls.

"Three-Zero-David give it up"

"You have a sick at 3515 Neptune cross street West 35 Street".

"Ten-four, do you now where it is"? Replies Brian

"Not sure let me look it up on the map. It is in the pit will take us a couple minutes to get there".

I hit the sixty-three button. That tells communications that we are responding. I turn on the lights and siren and we head to the job. Brian is copy down information from the computer on the job. We get there in three minutes.

We arrive on scene. I hit the eighty-eight button. That tells communications that we are on scene. There is a lady there.

She says "I do not feel well and can you take me to Coney Island Hospital"?

That is great I now where that hospital is. I start filling out the ambulance call report. Brian is asking her all the standard questions. He then takes her vital signs and calls them out to me.

"Pulse 88, respiration 16, blood pressure 132/78, normal across the board, no med. no allergies to med."

I record all the information on the report. I grab the stair chair and set it up. We place her in the chair and strap her in. We then roll her out to bus and lift her inside. Brian makes her conformable on the stretcher. I get in the driver's seat. Type HB forty-two in to the computer. That tells the dispatcher we are a basic life support ambulance and we are going to the hospital. We start heading to the hospital. I check the map we are crossing the correct street to the hospital. I can see the hospital in front of me and to the right.

We arrive at the hospital. I hit the eighty-one button. This tells the dispatcher we are at the hospital. We unload the patient and head in to the emergency room. I think to myself we did well on our first job by ourselves. We enter the emergency room. There are a couple of units in front of us waiting to be triage. Brian is finishing up the report on the patient.

It is now are turn to give a report on the patient and turn her over to the emergency room staff. The nurse signs the bottom of the report and we exit the emergency room. There are a couple of other ambulance crews outside talking as we exit the hospital.

"Hey how are you guys making out"? Somebody yells.

"We are doing pretty well" I reply.

We talk to the other crews for a couple of minutes. This is our first call together. Two rookies working the streets of New York together.

As the days go on we are getting better at reading the map and making U-turns with the ambulance. Coney Island Hospital is the only hospital we really now how to get to. So we try and convince all the patients to go there. Some of the patients will tell us they want to go to Maimonidies or Maymo as it is called in the street. We can never find this hospital so we just convince the patient that the hospital is closed to patients. That there are too many patients they're already. When it is foggy out. We will try and convince a patient that Victory Memorial Hospital is closed. I always use the towers of the Varrazzao Narrows Bridge as a guide to the hospital. The pit is fun to work in the summer. There are a lot of good-looking women running around.

It is a warm summer night. All the sudden the radio calls out.

"Three-Zero-David for the drug".

"Three-Zero-David send it".

"Three-Zero-David respond to the intox at the corner of West One Nine and Surf".

I hit the sixty-three button and we head on over to the job. Brian is driving and I am technician today. We arrive and there is a male intox on the corner. This is my first time meeting Sam. He is a regular that they talk about at the station. We walk up to him.

I ask him "Did you call an ambulance".

"Take me to Coney Island Hospital" he yells at us.

We help in to the back of the ambulance. He sits down on the bench seat. I put the seat belt on him. But he fights and takes it off. I finally get the seat belt on him. I am trying to get the information from him for the report.

"I am Sam take me to Coney Island Hospital" he yells again in the ambulance.

I have only two weeks in the field now. And I do not want to fill out the paperwork wrong and get in trouble.

"Sir I need your name for the report"

As I attempt to fill out the report as best as I can. We take off for the hospital. He stinks of cheap alcohol and body odor. In a couple of minutes we will be at the hospital. I have my face against the screen window to breathe. He stinks so badly. We finally get to the hospital. Brian goes and brings back a wheel chair. Sam gets up opens the doors and walks in to the hospital and lies on a stretcher. He does this like a professional. There are a couple of other ambulances there and a patrol supervisor.

"Oh I see you have meant Sam. He is one of the regulars down here. He calls for a bus every night. And he always wants to come to Coney". Somebody yells at us.

I am in the back of the bus spraying disinfected. When Brian comes out of the hospital. We have been at the hospital for twenty minutes. And it is time to go available. Or the dispatcher will start calling you.

"OK let's get out of here. I am thirsty lets stop by Seven-Eleven for a drink".

"Did you now that was Sam we picked up. They guy everybody talks about at the station".

"No well it was"

We are now heading toward seven-Eleven in an available status mode. We get there and there is another unit pulling out.

"Hey what do you want to drink"?

"I will take a Gatorade same here I will buy".

It is now about nine o'clock at night. The radio is quite. It seems as if everything went quite all at once. We have only two hours left on our shift. I hope it will be quite till I get off work at eleven o'clock. Well the end of the shift comes. We go back to the station and turn in our radios and run reports. I go in the locker room change out of my uniform and get ready to drive back to Long Beach. It will take me about an hour to get home.

"Hey Cali how is everything going"?

"OK"

"Brian is off today, so you are working with Rudy Biggs today; Do you now who he is"? The desk lieutenant tells me.

"Yes sir I worked with him the other day, Hey Rudy how is everything we are working together today".

"OK Cali you can drive I do not like to drive"

"OK let me get the map out this time"

We check out the ambulance and of course head to the store for something to drink. We get a sick job on the corner of Surf and Neptune. It is only a couple of blocks away. We arrive on the scene with in a couple of minutes.

There is a man on the corner and tells us he fells sick and wants to go to Victory Hospital. Rudy starts to evaluate the patient. I am copying down all the information on the call report. We are on the scene for maybe ten minutes. It is a clear night out so I can see the bridge in the distance. It will be no problem getting to the hospital. I take a real quick look at the map. Rudy is ready to go to the hospital. I type all the information into the computer. And we are off to the hospital.

All the sudden the computer goes blank in the ambulance. The next thing we hear is a message from the dispatcher that the computer system has gone down. We are unable to use the computers in the ambulances. And this is through out the entire city of New York. The radio is loud with different units calling the dispatcher. We now have to do all transmissions verbal. That's great I think to myself. I can see the hospital in the distance. I pull into the emergency room entrance. I pick up the radio to tell the dispatcher we are at the hospital. It takes a couple of minutes but I am finally able to get through.

"Three-Zero-David eighty-one at hospital forty-three"

"Got it" the dispatcher replies.

We take the patient into the emergency room. There is nobody in line. Rudy gives the report to the nurse. She signs for the patient and we are out of there in five minutes. We get back into the ambulance. You can hear the dispatcher reading jobs to units in the field. It is one job after another. After all Brooklyn is the busiest of the five boroughs. We are leaving the hospital I pick up the radio and tell the dispatcher we are available. I finally get through I tell her were available.

We head over to a restaurant that Rudy wants to eat out. The dispatcher is still reading jobs one after another over the radio. This goes on for four hours straight. We are lost in the system. I try to get through to her on the radio but it to busy. After a while I give up. Rudy goes in the restaurant and gets his food. I am not hungry yet. I look at my watch it is now about ten-thirty at night. We start heading back toward the station.

As we pull into the station the computer systems comes back up. We have about fifteen minutes left on the shift. We are told to log back on so the computer can logs us off by the Station Lieutenant. Rudy goes out to the bus and logs us on. The computer comes back in five minutes and logs us off for the shift. What a disaster I think to myself. The computer aided dispatch system is very important. I sign out and go home for the night.

I get to the station.

"Hey Cali you are working Three-One-Eddy for the next two weeks, You will be working with a female named Debbie Flack, Your bus will be back shortly, I will introduce you to her when she comes in at roll call" the lieutenant tells me.

"OK"

The unit sits at Surf and West 23 Street in the pit. Debbie is very nice and polite to work with. But she loves to change the radio station after each song. So you end up listening to all types of music. I check out the bus since I am the tech today. She put our numbers in the computer and we are signed on. We leave the station and head toward the pit. This is a slow unit not to busy. We talk and find out all the usual information on each other. We get to our location and park on one of the side streets. I pull out a book to read. She pulls out her gameboy and starts to play the game tetras.

"Three-One-Eddy for the assignment, you have an OB at 3112 Bayside Apartment A103 cross street Neptune" the radio calls out.

"Ten-four sixty-three"

I write down all the information on the call. Debbie starts driving to the call.

I tell her "I hate OB calls"

"No problem I will do the examination and patient care"

"Great thanks a lot"

We get to the scene in about two minutes. It is one of the large public housing complexes in the city. I grab my equipment. She grabs the stair chair and we head to the building. I look at the roofs to make sure nobody is throwing anything off the roof at us. We press the button and get buzzed in to the building.

We get to the apartment door. I listen everything sounds quite in the apartment. We knock on the door. A lady answers the door.

"Yea I called the ambulance, she is over on the couch in labor, and she needs to go to Coney Island Hospital" she tells us.

I start getting all the patient information. Debbie is doing the examination and patient care. All the sudden the door flies open. There is a tall black guy coming in the apartment yelling. He is cussing at the patient. It is her boyfriend. He tells us we are not taking her anywhere. He then yells at Debbie. At this point she grabs her radio.

"Three-One-Eddy ten-thirteen thirteen"

(The code ten-thirteen means need police emergency)

"The dispatcher calls back "Three-One-Eddy are you in danger"?

"Yes there is a guy in here violent with a gun send PD" she replies.

I turn the volume down on my radio. This is so the guy cannot hear what is going on. He has a small gun on him. And I do not want to get shot. You can hear other ambulances and supervisors responding over the radio. You can hear the sirens of the police cars responding. He has all in the living room and will not let us treat the patient. He has himself between the door and us. He is yelling that he does not want kids and she should have an abboritation. She is yelling back at him.

I try and move closer to the window. All you can see in the street is police cars and ambulances. They call the guy on the phone he answers and then hangs up. By this time he is really up set about what is going on. He is yelling how he should kill her. They call again and the guy hangs up. This goes on for a while they call he hangs up. By this time the Police Department Emergency Services Unit trucks start arriving. They have turned this in to a MCI (Mass Causality Incident). They are now classifying it as a hostage situation. The citywide Emergency Medical Service Chief is responding. The guy in the apartment is still very upset. I am trying to remain calm. All I want is a cigarette now. And I quite smoking along time ago.

This goes on for about two hours. He finally starts talking to a person on the phone. I do not now who it is. But this person is calming him down. Finally after about two hours he agrees to walk out of the apartment. At this point other crews and police rush in to the apartment.

"Are you two OK"? The lieutenant asks.

"I will be OK" I reply.

Debbie tells him she wants the counseling unit to respond to the station. The lieutenant tells another unit to transport the patient. He places us off service and returning to the station. It is about ten o'clock when we get back to the station. I am wondering if the job is worth it or not. I almost got shot tonight. I get off at eleven o'clock. All I want to do is go home and have a couple of beers.

The counseling unit arrives at the station. We go into a room and talk for a while. All I want to do is go home. We talk for about an hour. I am still thinking the whole time that I want a cigarette. I am trying not to smoke. Because I now I will probably start smoking again. They finally leave the station. No one knows what we talked about. It is now eleven thirty at night when I get done at the station. I sign out and head to my truck.

I decide that I am going to stop by Seven-Eleven on the way home. I go in and buy a Diet Coke and a pack of Newport cigarettes. I decide that I deserve a smoke and will try and quite at a later date. I feel more relaxed as I head back to Long Beach. When I get home I will have a couple of beers. I get home around midnight. The bars are still open. A couple of friends want me to meet them at a bar on Georgia Avenue. I decide to go out and have fun and relax. I now tomorrow will be another exciting day in the borough of Brooklyn.

I have now been on the job three months. It is starting to get cold out. I now New York gets a lot of snow. So as I am driving to work I think about transferring to Far Rockaway Queens. The station is about fifteen minutes from my apartment. I decide when I get to the station I will put the paperwork in to go to Far Rockaway. I go in the station and ask the desk lieutenant for the station transfer forms.

THE ARREST

Roll Call, Roll Call the public address system yells out. I go into the office.

"Cali you are being picked up today by Station Thirty-Three. You are working Thirty-Three-Frank, you partner is Geri Ross"

"OK Lieutenant Sutton".

I go get my equipment and go to the lounge and relax. It will be about thirty minutes before she gets hear.

She pulls up in one of the old Ford ambulances.

"Hi I am here to pick up my partner".

"He is in the lounge".

She comes in the lounge.

"Hi am I working with you"?

"I think so, is your name Geri Ross?

"Yes"

"That is whom I am supposed to work with".

"Hear is the keys, I do not drive" she replies.

"OK, Well I do not now Brooklyn, I have only been in New York fourteen weeks".

"Do not weary about it I will show you the way" she replies.

I grab my gear and take it out to and put it on the bus. I then get in the driver's seat. I have to adjust everything because Geri is small.

"OK do you need to get anything from the store"?

"Yea let's hit Seven-Eleven on Coney Island Avenue".

We log on to the computer and head toward our area.

We head over to Seven-Eleven on Coney Island Avenue. I go in and by a Diet Coke for myself and a Coke for Geri.

"Hey Cali hears the money for my Coke".

"No that's OK its on me, you can by me one later".

We start heading up Coney Island Avenue toward are area. We are talking about California and the job. When all the sudden we hear over the radio.

"Thirty-Three-Frank and Thirty-Three-Xray for the cardiac arrest".

"Thirty-Three-Frank send it over".

"You have a cardiac arrest at 810 Quintin Street on the third floor cross street Kings Highway".

"Ten-four, sixty-three".

I turn on the siren and lights and start heading up Coney Island Avenue. Geri is looking at the map. It is only about ten blocks from where we are. She is pulling up all the information on the computer. It tells use that the engine and medics are responding. The medic unit is from Maimonidies Hospital. It is one of the voluntary hospitals in the system. We get a message over the computer from the dispatcher. Fire is on scene CPR is in progress. I am getting ready to turn on to Kings Highway. It is now only a couple of blocks away. We can see the engine company lights. We pull up in front of the address. The medic unit pulls up behind us. I grab our oxygen and head into the building.

We go to the fourth floor and into the apartment. The engine company officer hands me the information on the patient. His wife is in the other room with the police officers. The patient has a good chance of survival. The medics hand me the keys to their ambulance.

He tells me "Bring up the scoop and set the stretcher on the first floor at the bottom of the stairs".

I run down the stairs thinking about what I have to do. I am really pumped up at this time. Most of my calls have been taxi rides to the hospital. Not real emergencies like this one. And I want to do the right thing.

I get to the ambulance and open the back doors. There scoop in under the bench seat. I grabbed the scoop and place it on top the stretcher. I then pull the stretcher dropping the wheels to the ground. I am moving as fast as I can. I roll the stretcher into the foyer. Garb the scoop and make a mad dash back up to the apartment. Their inside is the medics giving the patient life saving drugs. The firefighters are performing chest compressions and ventilating the patient. I can hear them counting one and two and three and four and five and breath yell the firefighter. The firefighter at the head then squeezes the bag forcing air into the patient's lungs.

The patient is tubed so there is no problem with his airway. Everytime the firefighter squeezes the ambo bag you can see the chest rise. This means that there is oxygen getting into the patient's lungs. And the circulation is accomplished by pressing on the patient's chest. My partner has gotten more information on the patient. The medics tell us to get ready to move the patient on the scoop and to be careful of the tube and the intravenous lines. We stop cardiopulmonary resuscitation and roll the patient on his side. I place the scoop to the side of the patient. We then roll the patient back on to his back on top of the scoop. The tube and intervenes lines are all in place and all right. We are now ready to move the patient down the stairs and to the ambulance.

We start to move the patient to the ambulance. It takes all eight of us to move him. We have to move him over the banister and down the stairs. All the time we are performing cardiopulmonary resuscitation on him. The lieutenant from the engine is coordinating the move. He would tell us when we were coming up to a corner and how to move the patient over the banister and down the next flight of stairs. Well we finally get the patient down to the first floor. Place him on the stretcher and wheel him out to the ambulance. Thirty-Three-Xray takes off for the hospital. They are going to Community Hospital of Brooklyn. It is a small hospital about ten blocks away.

All the sudden the lieutenant yells over the radio" Tell EMS to come back up to the apartment".

The firefighter relays the information to me. I ask what is the problem. He asks over the radio. The lieutenant tells him the wife is having a heart attack. I grab the oxygen tank and my technician bag and head to the apartment. There is a lady in her seventies sitting in a chair.

She is holding her chest and grasping for air. She is sweating and looks pale.

She tells me "I am having severe chest pain and I cannot breathe".

I place her on oxygen and take her vital signs.

I ask the lieutenant "Can you company hang around and help me out, I am all alone.

"OK we will stay, what do you need"?

"Thanks".

I get on the radio "Thirty-Three-Frank to Brooklyn South, Thirty-Three-Frank to Brooklyn South".

"Go ahead Thirty-Three-Frank".

"I need a medic unit for a cardiac".

"You have medics assigned" she replies.

"No they have left with the first patient in cardiac arrest, the patient's wife is having a cardiac, I am here all alone, send some help".

"Ten-four will send you help, I will send you Medics. Thirty-Three-Willie will be responding. I am also sending you Three-One-Boy to assist".

"Ten-four".

I ask the lieutenant to send one of his men to the bus to get the stair chair and a second oxygen bottle. I tell him that the chair is in the rear compartment. And the oxygen bottles are inside at the front of the bus. He tells the firefighter to get the equipment.

They get down and find the equipment and bring it back up. I now have the vital signs on the patient. The officer is filling out the ambulance call report for me. He writes down pulse 88 irregular, blood pressure 148 over 72 and respiration of 20, skin pale, clammy, and cool. We start loading the lady into the stair chair for the trip down to the ambulance. The firefighters are carrying the patient. I am carrying all my equipment. We get down to my ambulance. I can hear the other unit's sirens now. They are close now I feel a little relaxed.

Thirty-Three-Willie arrives on the scene. I tell them that the lady in back is complaining of chest pain and shortness of breath.

"OK we are going to move her to our bus".

Also Thirty-Two-Boy is on the scene now. I tell the Engine Company they can take up. The engine takes off for there station. The medics are in the back of their bus working on the patient.

"Hey Cali what hospital did they take her husband to"?

"They took him to Community Hospital of Brooklyn".

"OK that's where we will take her, Cali you can go ahead and leave for the hospital".

"Thanks for the back".

"Anytime"

I get in the ambulance and take off for the hospital.

I get to the hospital in about five minutes. There is Geri at the emergency Room entrance.

"Where have you been Cal"? She asks.

"Well the patient's wife became short of breath and had chest pains. The medics are bringing her in now" I reply.

Geri is finishing up her paperwork on our first patient. I head back to our ambulance to check the oxygen and put the ambulance back in service. In a couple of minutes the medics arrive with the wife. She looks better now. They wheel her into the emergency room. She ask the nurse how is her husband is doing. She thanks us and is pushed into the treatment room. Geri tells me her husband will survive and that I am getting a prehospital save bar on medial day. I always wanted one. The prehospital save bar is red and yellow red stripes. It means that you saved a person in cardiac arrest.

We get in our ambulance and head to our area. It is in a different part of Brooklyn. And of course a new experience for me. The area is mostly five stories, old apartment buildings. And they are all walk ups no elevators. We are sitting in the bus just talking about California and New York and how the two areas are alike and different. Geri is a lot of fun to work with.

All the sudden we hear "Thirty-Three-Frank for the assignment, you have a sick job at 3415 Bedford Avenue, Cross Street Avenue O".

"Ten-four sixty-three"

Geri starts to write down the information. I press the sixty-three button. We then pull up the MR on the computer. It tells us that there is an elderly lady there that feels sick and dizzy. I turn on the lights and siren and start heading for the call. It is a couple of blocks from the previous job. So I know where I am going. And of course it is a five-story walkup. And yes the patient is on the fifth floor. I think these people have got to be in good shape to walk up and down the stairs these stairs everyday.

We get in to the apartment. There is an elderly lady sitting in a chair with her husband close by.

"What is the problem, why did you call the ambulance"? Geri ask

"I feel real sick to my stomach and very dizzy" she replies

"Do you have any medical problems we should now about"?

The lady starts tell us her medical history. I am writing all the information down on the ambulance call report. Then her husband hands me basket with all her medications in it. There has to be at least twenty different types of medications. I start writing all them down. I run out of space and have to use the bottom comments section to fit them all in.

Geri starts taking the lady's vital signs. And then she calls them out to me.

"Pulse 72, Blood pressure 138/76, Repirations 16, Normal across the top".

I write them all down. Then I unfold the stair chair. We place the lady in the chair and strap her in. she is not real heavy and we can carry her down without assistance. I am out the top and counting. It is only five flights down with a hallway in between each flight. We get her out to the bus. She tells us she will only go to Coney Island Hospital. I get in the driver's seat. Geri climbs in the back. We take off for the hospital. It will only take about ten minutes to get there. The patient is stable so it is not an emergency. This is what must of our calls are like in the city of New York. After the job we head back to our area. The rest of the night is uneventful. It is getting close to time to head back to the station to drop me off.

"Hey Geri I need a ride back to my station".

"No problem Cal, Go down Kings Highway till you get to Ocean Parkway and turn right. Take it down to Coney Island Hospital. The hospital will be on the left". She replies.

"That should be easy"

We start heading back to the station.

"Hey Geri it was great working with you"

"It's been fun working with you to" she replies.

She drops me off at the station. I go in and sign off duty for the night. I will be off for the next three days. It will be nice. I am planing on going down to Philadelphia to see my parents and hang out with some friends. It will be a fun filled three days off.

Well my days off are over. It is now time to go back to work. I throw my gear in my truck and start heading to the station. It will take me forty-five minutes to get there. I am getting to now Brooklyn pretty good. I can get to most of the hospitals without much trouble. I am also able to find most of the major streets without a problem. I arrive at the station about fifteen minutes before my shift. I put on my uniform and grab my gear. I now ready for roll call.

I am working with Barry tonight. We check out the ambulance and log on to the computer. We head out of the station and over to Seven-Eleven to get something to eat and drink. We are getting ready to head to our area when we get our first job. It is a fire standby in the Gravesend Homes projects. I now it is located down in the pit. Plus all we have to look for is all the fire equipment on the scene. I turn on the emergency lights and siren and start heading toward the area.

Barry is looking on the map to make sure we are going the correct way. We arrive at the scene within a couple of minutes. There is a fire on the fourth floor of the building. The Battalion Chief tells us they are bringing out a couple of people overcome by smoke. I get ready to give Brooklyn South a ten-twelve. That is the code for a scene report.

I pick up the mike "Three-Zero-David to Brooklyn South with a ten-twelve".

"Go ahead Three-Zero-David"

"We have a high-rise fire, with fire on the number four floor in one apartment. Fire is brining us down at least two patients. Staging will be on Neptune and West Three One Street. Can I have additional unit".

"Ten-four Three-Zero-David, Three-Zero-David switch to Citywide, Also you have a patrol boss responding"

"Three-Zero-David ten-four"

We can hear more sirens in the background. About that time we see a patrol boss arrive on the scene. It is lieutenant McNash. I feel a lot better that he is on scene and in charge. He tells us that we are going to be the treatment sector and will not be transporting. There are two more units assigned to transport. That makes me feel even better. The firefighters finally bring us the two patients. They are two women both overcome by smoke. They are conscious and choking on the smoke. We place them both on the bench seat and give them oxygen. Barry starts taking vital signs. I start taking down all the information for the Ambulance Call Report. About that time two more ambulances arrive on scene. They will be the transport units.

"What do you guys have"?

"We have two patients overcome by smoke".

"OK are they ambulatory"?

"Yes"

"All right we will put them in our bus".

I give them the copies of the Ambulance Call Report.

The firefighters are starting to take up. This means we will be available in a couple minutes. We have been at the fire for two hours. There are no more patients. We start putting our equipment away and wait for the lieutenant to release back to service.

Lieutenant McNash tells us "Take up and go back into service. You two did a good job here tonight".

"Thanks sir"

It is now half way through our shift. We start heading back toward our area. It is up near King Highway and Ocean Avenue in Brooklyn.

"Well that job went pretty good," I say.

"Yea considering it was our first three-alarm fire with patients" Barry replies.

It is getting close to the end of our shift. We have not had any other calls. I am thinking of my drive home tonight. It is a nice night out and I think I will go for a run on the boardwalk when I get home. We start heading back to the station for the end of shift. We have to turn in our paperwork. The desk lieutenant will go over to make sure it is correct. If anything needs correcting we will do it now before it goes downtown to headquarters.

He tell us "The paperwork is correct, and have a nice night"

"Good by sir"

The next three days Barry will be off. I have no idea who I will be working with.

"Hey Cali I need to talk to you".

"Yes sir"

"There is a permanent slot for you on Three-Zero-David tour three on a platoon do you want it"?

"Yes sir"

"OK your new schedule will be a platoon tour three".

"Yes sir no problem"

"You will start the schedule next Sunday; it is the being of the month"

I think to myself that will be great. I can now figure out my schedule for the year. It will be easier to do mutual. That is working two tours and single, and then being off for four and five days. I will also now whom I am working with all the time. It is a tactical unit so I will be going all over the city.

BROOKLYN EXPERENCE

I have now been on the job three months. It is very interesting and a great experience. I am starting to now my way around Coney Island and Brooklyn South without much trouble. I have gotten to now the people I work with. They are a great group and very helpful. I really like my assignment. I have kept in touch with some of my classmates from the academy. I am thinking of all this as I drive to work. It takes me about forty-five minutes. I arrive at the station thirty minutes before my shift.

I put my uniform on and report to the desk lieutenant.

"Hey Cali"

"Hi sir what am I doing today"?

"You are detailed to the Woodhull Station; Do you now where that is"?

"No sir"

"It is not that hard to find, it is Off-Broadway, Take the GMC Jimmy and go there".

"Yes sir".

So I head out of the station. And of course I stop by Seven-Eleven for a Diet Coke for the trip. I am headed to an area called Brooklyn North. I have never been here before.

It has been an hour since I left the station. I have found Broadway. When the radio calls out my vehicle number on the Citywide Channel. It is Jeff Ames. He is a captain at the citywide desk.

He asks me "Where are you at"?

I reply "on Broadway near Elmhurst Hospital".

He replies "You are in Queens how did you do that".

A message appears on the computer. I am to call the citywide desk. I call; Jeff gives me the directions to Woodhull. He explains to me that there is a Broadway in all the boroughs of New York. I make a u turn. It takes me about another forty-five minutes to get there.

I enter the station. The desk lieutenant is they're waiting for me.

"You must be Cali, what happen? You are working with John Featherstone" he tells me.

"I got a little lost sir, I do not now this area" I reply.

John and I talk I find out he has been on the job twenty-five years, and has been working in this area for the last twenty years. I think to myself dam this guy has some time on the job. He tells me I am driving and he will give me directions to the jobs and the hospital. I feel secure working with him. We shake hands and head out to the ambulance.

We are getting ready to the leave the station. When the radio starts calling us and the computer lights up with a job. We are to respond to a cardiac arrest at 307 Hart Street, the cross street is Lewis. And that Thirty-Six-Xray is the paramedic unit responding with us.

"That is easy to get to; it is about five blocks from the station" John replies.

John gives me the directions. We get there in about two minutes. It is a five-story walk up. And the patient is on the fifth floor. This will be a tough job. I grab all the equipment and head up the stairs.

The paramedics have not arrived yet. The family is yelling for us to hurry up. It is their grandfather. We enter in to this small bedroom. The patient is lying on the bed. There is not much room to work. Due to there is so much stuff stored in the room. John is right behind me as we enter the room. I can hear the paramedics coming down the street. I start moving stuff out of the way. So we can out the patient on the floor and start chest compressions. He is a small frame man. He is not too heavy.

John hooks up the defibrillator. I place an airway in the patient's mouth. So the tongue will not get in the way. I place the pads on the patient's chest. John presses the analyze button. The machine will tell us when to shock the patient. It is designed to shock the heart back in to a normal rhythm. The machine tells us to clear the patient and then gives the patient a shock. The patient moves a little. I check for a pulse at the patient's neck and feel nothing. John then presses the analyze button again. The defibrillator then shocks the patient again. Again I feel no pulse after the shock. We do this three times. This is per our protocol. I then start chest compressions on the victim. John starts squeezing the ambo bag after I do five compressions.

The paramedics are entering the apartment now.

"Do you guys have any information on the patient"? They ask.

"No"

"Cali, go get the information, we will take over".

I take the family in to the livingroom. I ask her to get me his medications and his insurance card. She comes back with his card and medications. I start copying down all the information.

"His name is John Doe, he is sixty-five years old, and he had a physical two months ago and is in good health per his doctor"

"Ok we are doing all we can for him now "I tell her

I go back in to the bedroom. The paramedics are still working on him on the floor. They have put a tube in his throat and given him all the medications that are required for a person in cardiac arrest. There is still no change in his condition. We are still doing compressions and breathing for him. The paramedics have asked for the phone. He is going to call the fire department doctor and ask for permission to stop. We have now been in the apartment for about thirty minutes working on the patient. The monitor shows a straight line. There is no heart activity at all.

The paramedic comes back into the room. He tells us that telemetry has given permission to stop. He then goes and tells the daughter what is going on. We place the patient back in bed. Remove the intravenous lines and the tube from his throat. He now looks like he is sleeping. We now start to clean up the area. Place all the disposal equipment in a red bag for disposal. This is for disposal at the station since it is all considered infectious waste.

We head back to the station John and I do not talk a lot. He has been on the job for a long time. We take the defibrillator into the station lieutenant. John starts filling out all the paperwork. He comes back out to the ambulance we decide to go to Seven-Eleven to get something to drink. It is starting to close to the time for me to head back to my station. When all the sudden we get a call for an emotionally disturbed person (EDP).

"All shit I should be heading back to Station thirty-one to go home" I say.

The radio calls out "Thirty-Six-Adam for the EDP"

"Thirty-Six-Adam give it up".

"You have an EPD on 182 Vernon Ave cross street Thompkins, Be careful he is violent" the dispatcher tells us.

It appears on the screen. It also tells us that police are not assigned to the call yet. It is not far from the station and it will take us about five minutes to get there. When we arrive the police are on the scene. And the patient has been restrained.

"He has been smoking crack and drinking" the police tell us.

Ok we put in the bus. John gets in back and starts copying down all the information. We have been on the scene for about ten minutes.

"OK Cali, take him over to Woodhull Hospital" John yells from the back of the bus.

Cool that is where the station is located. We can get the patient signed for. I park the ambulance and head back to Coney Island. And I will still get off work at 2300 hours I think.

We start out for the hospital. It takes me five minutes to get there. I pill up the ramp to the emergency room. We take the patient inside. He smells real bad and is very dirty.

"What do you guys have?" The triage nurse asks.

"We have an EDP that is on crack and drinking" I reply.

"Ok put him over there"

She signs the ambulance call report. We head out to the bus. I want to get out of hear fast. We go around the corner to the station. The desk lieutenant has put us out if service.

I stop by the station and turn in my radio and keys.

"Ok Cali you can head back to Station thirty-one, Do you now how to get there"? The lieutenant replies.

"Yes sir it should take me about thirty to forty-five minutes to get there".

"OK, do not get lost" the Lieutenant replies.

"I will not"

I leave and head out to the Jimmy. I can not wait to get back to my station. Station thirty-six is ok but I would not want to work there.

I get to my station with about ten minutes left in my tour.

"Hey Cali go ahead and sign out and go home" Lieutenant Smith tells me.

"No problem sir thanks a lot see you tomorrow" I reply.

I head into the locker room put my equipment in my locker change into a pair of jeans and head to my truck. I get home in about forty-five minutes. I go in my apartment watch a little television and go to bed. I have to work my part-time job tomorrow since the city pays so well.

"Hey Cali you are working with a new guy today. He just got out of the academy. His name is Charlie" the lieutenant tells me.

"Ok I am going to check out the bus"

There is a new guy sitting in the lounge.

I ask him "Are you Charlie"?

"Yes"

"OK I am Cali we are working together today I see the bus is over there, OK you want to start checking out the bus, I will log us on with the computer."

You can always tell a new guy. They count everything before they check the box on the eight hundred form. It is thirty minutes into the shift. We are getting ready to leave for are area. All the sudden the radio calls out.

"Thirty-Three-David for the assignment"

"Thirty-Three-David give it up".

"Respond to 2401 West Street third floor for the injury minor"

"Ten-four sixty-three".

I think oh well this is another taxi ride to the hospital. I want to stop and get something to eat, I am hungry. We arrive in front of the building in about five minutes. Charlie grabs his equipment. I grab the stair chair and head to the third floor of the building. It is a walk up there is no elevator. And with my luck it will be some heavy person. We get to the third floor. And there the patient is on the floor.

There is a boy about six years old on the floor. He has the handle bar and hand brake lever stuck in his thigh area. It is through the skin and inbreeded in his thigh. Well this is no normal taxi ride. Charlie looks at me. I am thinking what we should do. I start to examine the boy. He is not crying at all.

He tells me "It hurts a little but that is it."

As I examine the wound you can see the femoral artery in his leg pulsating. The femoral artery is a major artery in the leg. You can bleed to death in couple of minutes by injuring it. This is no normal call I think to myself.

I get on the radio "Thirty-Three-David to Brooklyn South".

"Go ahead Thirty-Three-David".

"We need fire or ESU; we have a six year old male with a handle bar in his thigh, also send a medic unit."

"Ten-four".

The super of the building shows up. He has brought his toolbox with him. He asks if he can help.

I tell him "I need a screwdriver and an adjustable wrench. Charlie go get a backboard and at least four extra straps".

We are going to have to take the handle bar off the bicycle. Then we will have to transport both to the hospital. A couple of minutes have gone by. I am trying to get the handle bar off the bike. You can hear the fire equipment sirens in the distance. They should be here soon. The sirens go silent. I now they are in front of the building. And will be here in a couple of minutes to help.

The officer from the truck arrives on the floor.

"What do we have?"

"We have the handle bar stuck in his thigh. But the bigger problem is. It is right next to the femoral artery. We have to be careful not to touch the artery."

"OK"

He tells his men to bring up the toolbox. We start to take the handle bar off the bike. One firefighter is supporting the child. And one is holding the handle bar. It takes us about fifteen minutes to get the handle bar free from the bike.

The next thing to do is to secure the boy and the handle bar to the backboard. The medics have arrived and are starting a line the boy. This is going to take some engineering. We start securing the boy to the board being very careful not to move the handle bar in any way. This takes us about thirty minutes to do. Then will come the fun part, getting him down all the stairs. We finally get him secured to the board.

It is time for the stairs. All the firefighters and police get on the stairs. The decision is made to pass the board over the banister on each flight of stairs. This will take a while. But it is the best way to keep him secured. Also on each landing all knots and rigging will be checked to see if still secure. This takes a good thirty minutes. We finally get the child out to the ambulance. The medics are in the back doing their advance life support procedures on the child. His mother is at work. The police are getting all the information to go get the mother. They will meet us at the hospital. We tell the police we will be going to Lutheran Hospital Trauma Center. We have now been on the scene about an hour. I think to myself this was really was not an injury minor call. This should have been a trauma job. The medics tell me go ahead and start out for the hospital.

I tell them "Hey it has been a long time since I have been to Lutheran Hospital. Let me follow you there."

"OK follow us, we will give the notification".

I hear them give the hospital notification. It takes us about five minutes to get to the hospital. I pull in and then back into the emergency room entrance. There are a couple of people waiting outside and looking at the patient. The trauma team is waiting for us in the trauma room. We carefully remove the boy from the ambulance and head to the trauma area. Once in the room the doctor starts asking the medics all sorts of questions.

The x-ray technician enters the room to take x-rays of the wound. He places the x-ray films up to the light. You can see the handle bar inside the patient's leg. He is still secured to the backboard. There is a group of doctors looking at the x-rays and discussing the patient. They finish their discussion. They come over to the patient and tell him something. They give him a shot to numb the area. Then they remove all the straps. All the sudden the primary trauma surgeon pulls the handle bar out of the leg. He tells us it was close to the femoral artery, and that we did a great job of securing it and transporting him to the hospital.

I am thinking to myself damn that kid was lucky. I head back out to the bus. And start cleaning up all the mess in the back. That is my job since I am the driver. My partner is still inside getting information and writing the report.

Charlie comes out says "Hey I am ready whenever you are, that was an interesting call."

I reply "Yea that is one for the book. This is the type of call where you have to put all your street experience you have together to treat the patient. I bet they never taught you that in the academy."

"No they don't teach you that."

We start heading back to Coney Island. That is where we are assigned. It is now about three hours into my six-hour overtime shift.

"Hey stop somewhere and get something to drink".

"Sure where do you want to go? Good old Seven-Eleven".

"Sure why not there is one down the street on the corner".

We leave the store Charlie is still talking about the last job we had. He is new on the job. He has only been in the field about three weeks. I generally don't like to work with new people. This is because you have to keep an eye on them all the time. But Charlie is different he can think for himself and does not act like he knows everything. We get back to our area and stop by the station. We have to get a backboard and replace some other supplies. We stock the bus and head to Coney Island Beach. That is where we are supposed to sit.

It is great getting paid overtime to look at all the women in their bathing suits. Some look hot and others will make you sick. We stand outside the bus just looking and talking about the view. I have about two hours left on the tour. When we get the second call of the shift.

"Thirty-Three-David for the injury on the beach. You have an eighteen-year-old female with a fractured right ankle. The lifeguard will guide you to her" the dispatcher tells use.

"Thirty-Three-David ten-four"

We head over to the area where she is reported to be. There is a lifeguard they're waving at us. We walk through the sand to where she is. There is a hot looking female.

"I think I broke my ankle "she tells us.

"No problem"

Charlie begins to examine the ankle. It is swollen and deformed. She tells us it hurts to move it. Charlie is putting a pillow splint on the ankle. I am getting all the information for the report. She has a nice tan and is very polite in giving the information. Charlie finally gets done putting the splint on her ankle. We put her in the chair and start to carry her out to the bus. She is not heavy so it will not be that bad. We finally get her to the bus help her up inside and place her on the bench seat.

I ask her "Do you want to go to Coney Island Hospital"?

"Sure can you take me there"?

"Sure, Hey Charlie, are you ready"?

"Yea go eighty-two to hospital forty-two".

I type all the information and the mileage into the computer. The computer now shows us going to the hospital. We start out for the hospital. I can hear Charlie talking to the patient in the back of the ambulance. He appears to have a good conversation going on with her. We arrive at the hospital. It was a five-minute ride.

I go in and get a wheelchair for her. We help her into the wheelchair. Charlie grabs the handle and starts pushing her into the emergency room. All the time they are still talking. It appears he is going to get a date with her. He takes her over to the triage desk and gives the nurse a report. She signs the ambulance call report. Charlie has a big smile on his face when I see him.

"Hey I got a date with her, I hooked up, She lives near me" he tells me.

"Cool, hey lets take it in overtime personnel, my six hours is almost up"

"OK"

"Thirty-Three-David going in overtime personal".

"Ten-four Thirty-Three-David thanks for the help".

We head back to the station. It is around the corner from the emergency room.

I fill out my overtime sheet and get the lieutenant to sign it.

"I'll see you around Cali" Charlie yells.

"Hey we will have to work some overtime together soon".

"All right that would be great; maybe we should work lower Manhattan. They say there are a lot of good looking women running around there".

"OK see you around" Charlie replies.

TRANSFER TO QUEENS

It is getting close to winter in New York. I have made it through my probation period. I am now an employee of the New York City Emergency Medical Service. I think I will go out and party tonight with a couple of friends to celebrate. It has been a long time since I have driven in snow. I think I will transfer to Far Rockaway. It is only about fifteen minutes from my house. It will be pretty cool working down on the beach all summer long. The draw back is it gets pretty cold in the winter. The cold air blows off the ocean, and you freeze.

I go into the station.

"Hey Lieutenant Stone, can I get a request for transfer form?"

"Sure where do you want to go?" he asks.

"The Rockaways Station 41 in Queens".

"You are going to freeze down there in the winter".

"I will survive sir."

"Ok here is your form"

I take the form into the lounge and fill it out. I then take it back to the lieutenant.

A couple of months go by. I do not hear anything. Then in December, I come down on orders to report to Station 41 in Rockaway Queens. I call the station and talk to Lieutenant Mitch. He tells me he is the scheduling officer.

"What tour do you want?"

"I would like tour three sir".

"Ok you will work tour three at fifteen hundred hours. You report on Monday at fifteen hundred hours. You are assigned to Four-Zero-Boy Three a new tactical unit in Queens." He tells me.

"No problem sir, see you Monday".

I get to the station a little early on Monday. I meet the desk lieutenant.

"Hello my name is James Thompson I am assigned here now sir.

"Ok go in the locker room and try and find you a locker" he tells me.

I go into the locker room. I able to find a locker, I put my gear in the locker and secure it. At least I do not have to drive around with my gear in my truck. I head back into the office.

"Here is some paperwork I need you to fill out. Go in the lounge and fill it out and bring it back".

It is just the normal station forms. I bring the forms back into the office. By now most of the tour three personal are coming into the station.

Roll call Roll call over the station public address system. Everybody goes into the office.

"Good afternoon everybody"

"Good afternoon Lieutenant Mitch"

"We have a new man assigned the station. His name is James Thompson everybody calls him Cali. He is assigned to Four-Zero-Boy on the mainland. You will be working with Frank."

"Ok sir thanks" I reply.

I grab my gear and head out to the ambulance.

"Hey you can drive I have no idea where anything is in Queens other then the Academy".

"No problem what is your shield number to log on?"

"It is 1234"

"Got it we are logged on"

I am still checking out the back of the bus. This way I will now where all the equipment is.

"Are you ready to go to the mainland?"

"Yea you can head up there"

That is what they call the main part of Queens. Rockaway is an island that is connected by two bridges.

We start heading toward the bridge to take to the mainland.

"Do you want to stop and get something to drink?"

"Yea shore"

We stop at a deli. I pick up a Diet Coke and Frank gets a Coke.

"We go to hospital thirty-six most of the time".

"Ok just tell me if we go to another hospital"

We pull into a city park and park. It is a pretty nice area. You can not see us from the street. So people can not ask us directions or a lot of questions. Frank tells me this is where we sit. That it is not a bad area. We are talking he tells me he is going to the police department soon. That he will be leaving in the next three months. Then we start talking about motorcycles.

"What you ride?"

"Yea I have a Honda Shadow" Frank replies.

"That's cool I have a Kawasaki Ninja, Lets go for a ride sometime".

"Where do you live?"

"In the city of Long Beach on Long Island. It is about fifteen minutes from the station."

All the sudden the radio calls out "Four-Zero-Boy, Four-Three-Xray for the arrest, 103 street and Lefferts Boulevard".

"Four-Zero-Boy give it up"

The job appears on the computer screen. It is a cardiac arrest on 103 Street and Lefferts Boulevard. It is a street job. There is a male lying on the sidewalk. I think to myself that it is probably an intox. Frank turns on the siren and lights. We start heading to the job. We are about ten blocks from the job. Four-Three-Xray is closer that they should get there before us. We get there in about four minutes. They are already on the scene and have the patient in the back of their bus. It is an intox and they will transport.

"You guys can eighty-seven the call" they tell us.

We are now clear the job and back in service. It is now twenty-two-forty-five hours. It is time to head back to the station. We get back to the station and call it a day. It is a lot different then working Brooklyn. The desk lieutenant checks all your paperwork. I change my clothes and head home for three days off.

"Hey Cali for the next couple of days you are going to work with Lee McCall on Four-One-Adam".

"Yes sir"

"Hi, I am Lee. You must be Cali; we are working together for the next couple of days. You drive so you can learn the area".

It is not a hard are to learn. If you go in three directions you hit water. Lee is a big guy. I would not want to get him mad. There is a lot of public housing in the Rockaways. I feel safe working with him. Lee has a very heavy accent when he talks. But I can understand him.

"We do two to three jobs a shift. Nothing major, it gets very cold down here in the winter. You can feel the wind off the ocean." He tells me.

They were right, it dose get cold down here. But it is also close to the house so I will not complain. I will just deal with it. The next night I will tech and Lee will drive. I head home after the shift. It is nice only taking fifteen minutes to get home. And there is no traffic to deal with. I like it a lot.

I go into the station the next shift. There is Lee sitting in the lounge waiting for the unit to come back from a late job.

"Hi James, They should be back in thirty minutes," he says to me.

"Ok, Hey Lee how are you doing" I reply.

I sit down and watch some television. Lee always calls me by my proper name. I guess that is the way he I think to myself.

We get are first of job of the shift.

The radio calls out "Forty-One-Adam for the sick at Seven Eleven Seagirt. You have a lady the states she does not feel well".

The job comes up on the computer. I copy down all the information on the back of the report. Lee turns on the lights and we start heading to the call. It takes about three minutes to get there. We enter the apartment. There is a lady walking around.

"Hi did you call the ambulance?"

"Yea I called the ambulance. I do not feel well and want to go to Peninsula General Hospital only".

"Ok can you explain to me how you feel".

She starts to explain. Lee is copying down all medication and insurance information. I take her vital signs and get all her information for the report. We put her in the stair chair and start heading to the ambulance.

"James we are going to hospital number thirty-seven".

"Ok thanks".

We put here on the stretcher and place her in the back of the ambulance. We start heading to the hospital. It takes us about ten minutes to get there. I am filling out the call report on the way to the hospital. We get to the hospital. The report is filled out. Unload the patient and wheel her in to the emergency room. I see the triage nurse and give her the report. She tells us what area to put the patient in and signs the report. I give the clerk the copies and head back out to the ambulance.

"James can I please see the ACR"? Lee asks me.

He makes me feel like I do not now what I am doing. I have been on the job a little over a year now. We pull away from the emergency room entrance. And park the ambulance in the back part of the parking lot. No body has ever called me on my paperwork before.

"Why"? I ask.

"Because if you make a mistake on it we both get in trouble"

He is very loud and his size makes me nervous. I hand him the paperwork. He is checking all the boxes and the comment section. He starts showing me all the little mistakes I made.

"Would you please correct the mistakes," He asks me.

I am thinking to myself that I have to work with this guy for the next two weeks. This is going to be a pain in the ass. After every call we go on. Lee has to check my paperwork. It gets to the point where I just hand him the report after each job. As the days go by there is less and less mistakes he can find. It finally gets to the point to the point where he cannot find any mistakes. Well ten years later still on the job. I use this information he taught me. I am still grateful for his time and patients with me. It has kept me out of trouble. And I have received complements on my paperwork from other officers.

I see Frank at the station.

"Hey Cali I got hired by the police department. Tomorrow is my last day at the station" He tells me.

"Hey good luck see you around" I reply.

I wonder whom I will be working with. Frank was a lot of fun. And we would go for long motorcycle rides after work to relax.

"Hey Cali you are going to have new partners they are Frank Barnes and Oscar Smith" Lieutenant Mitch tells me.

"Ok sir" I rely.

I wonder how these two guys are to work with. I have scene them around the station. But I have never worked with them. I know that Oscar is going to school for nursing. And that Frank is on Tour One. It is my first day of working with Frank. He tells he is married and has four dogs. We talk to each other and get to now each other. We start heading up to our area in the park. We are talking about different things. You could say we are seeing what each of us is like.

We get our first job. The radio calls us and the job appears on the screen. Four-Zero-Boy unknown condition at the Whitestone Bridge. The only other information we have is that PD and PDESU are responding. I am driving and Frank is teching. I look up on the area up on the map. Frank writes down all the information on the report. We start heading toward the bridge. I have my lights and siren on.

"Four-Zero-Boy PD is calling for a rush and they changed the job to a trauma" the dispatcher tells us.

I am proud of myself I now where I am going finally. Queens is very confusing to learn I think.

When all the sudden at 167 street and 32 Avenue. I hear a loud nose. All the sudden the ambulances swerves off the road flips over and hits a tree. There is a red sports car sitting in the middle of the intersection.

"Frank are you alright"? I ask

"No my shoulder and back hurt" he replies.

"My chest hurts real bad." I tell him.

"Four-Zero-Boy to Queens we have been involved in a major vehicle accident at 167 Street and 32 Avenue. We are trapped in the bus" Frank tells the dispatcher.

"Ten-Four I will send you help" the dispatcher replies.

I feel real dizzy and do not remember everything that happened. All the sudden we can hear the sirens of vehicles coming to help us. I feel a little bit better now knowing help is on the way. The next thing I know, there are chiefs, police, ambulances, an Engine Company and Ladder Company on the scene.

The Ladder Company is having trouble getting the doors open. You can hear them cutting and the metal ripping as they work to free us. I can feel the door start to open. Then come the paramedics with the long board, collars, and stretcher. They start getting Frank and I out of the ambulance. I am pretty sore and banged up. They are also treating the driver of the other car.

They start asking me all the usual questions.

"Are you on any medications; are you allergic to any medications"?

"No" I reply.

"What happen"?

"I do not remember the accident. All I actually remember is Frank calling Queens and telling them about the accident" I reply.

"We are taking you to Elmhurst Hospital Trauma Center in Queens. There is a chief and a lieutenant they're waiting for you".

They are writing down all the information and filling out paperwork. The police department is there taking down information and filling out their paperwork. Then all the sudden there is a girl screaming.

"Where is the asshole driving the ambulance?"

She is trying to get the back doors open on the ambulance and get in. She is yelling that her car is totaled. The police come over and pull her away from the ambulance. She is yelling at them. They finally arrest her for interfering with government operation.

The paramedics have an intravenous in me. I am on a monitor. They start out for the hospital. There is a police car in front of us. As we rush to the hospital I can hear the siren and feel the movement of the bus. It feels different being the patient. Not the driver or the technician in back. Frank is in a different ambulance. It takes us about five minutes to get to the hospital. They back up to entrance pull the stretcher out and drop the wheels. I can feel them pushing fast into the trauma room. The hospital is waiting for us. The paramedic is giving his report to the trauma team. I cannot understand what he is saying. They put me on the trauma stretcher. The trauma doctor starts giving orders.

"I want a complete set of x-rays of the head, chest, abdomen, also CAT scan the head," he yells.

The nurse calls and makes all the arraignments. I have not scene Frank yet to see how he is doing.

"Hello I am Doctor Smith what happen"?

"We got hit at an intersection and the bus flipped over. My chest hurts and I have a real bad headache sir".

"Any loss of consciousness"?

"I might have been knocked out for a minute. I really do not remember the accident sir".

"Ok we are going to get some pictures and do a CAT scan of your head".

"Ok".

I see Frank at the X-ray department. He is on another stretcher. He does not look too bad.

"Hey Cali how do you feel"?

"I got one hell of a headache and my chest still hurts how about you Frank"?

"My shoulder is still sore that's about it"

"Ok, well I guess we are off for a couple of days".

"Yea it looks that way".

In comes Lieutenant Olock. He is doing the accident report.

"You were driving correct"? He asks.

"Yes sir".

"What happen"?

"Well sir we were headed north bound on 32 Avenue. We had our siren and lights on. I saw that the interaction was clear and started to enter the interaction. When all the sudden I heard a loud noise and the vehicle flipped over. That is all I remember sir".

"Ok that is how I will put it in the report".

Doctor Smith comes into the room.

"Well it looks like you have a couple of contusions nothing serious. You will be off for the next couple of days. You can get dressed now. I will get your discharge papers ready".

"Great one problem they cut my uniform off me in the field" I reply.

"Ok I will get you a pair of pajamas to put on to go back to your station" he replies.

Frank has a sprained shoulder. We will both be off on line of duty injury for the next couple of days. That means you are stuck in the house all day.

We leave the hospital and head to the station. It takes about forty-five minutes to get back to Rockaway. Lieutenant Olock has already gotten our gear off the bus. We get to the station. I put on some clothes and get ready to go home. Lieutenant Olock will drive us home. I now I will be stuck in the house for the next couple of days. That is really going to suck.

Well I have been off on line of duty injury for the last five days. I have to go see the department doctor today. I get ready to drive to Manhattan. That is where the medical office is. It will take me about an hour to get there. And of course it is a pain in the ass to find parking. I finally find a parking place. I go downstairs and sign in at the medical office. There are a couple guys there in front of me. We are all talking about different things on the job. They finally call my name. I answer and go in and see the doctor.

"How are you feeling"? He ask

"I feel fine and want to go back to work sir" I rely.

"Ok you can return to work tomorrow" he replies.

"Great thanks see you sir".

I am out of the office and on my way home. I cannot wait to get back to the station. It gets real boring sitting around the house all day.

"Holy shit it is cold out" I say.

As I get out of bed. Well it is winter in wonderful New York City. You can feel the cold wind blowing off the ocean. I start getting ready for work. I know it will be a cold shift today. And I hate cold weather. That is why I loved living in California. It is always warm out there. Well I live in New York now. So I will have to get use to the cold winters. I run outside and let my truck warm up while I get ready for work. There are a couple inches of snow on the ground already. My truck warms up and I start out for work. It might take me a little longer to get there. It takes me about thirty minutes to get to the station. But I make it there without a problem. Pretty good for somebody that has not driven in the snow.

I arrive at the station.

"Hey Cali you're working with Mike Clark today on Four-Three-Adam in Howard Beach on the main land" the desk lieutenant tells me.

"That should be interesting sir" I reply.

Mike does not like to drive. So I will have to drive in the snow. We start out for the mainland. I am driving slow trying to get use to the snow. The ambulance is slipping and sliding around. All the sudden the radio calls use for a job.

"Four-Three-Adam for the assignment. You have an injury major at 1034 101 Ave. dog mulled a teenage boy" the dispatcher tell us.

"Four-Three-Adam ten-four".

We start heading to the job siren and lights on. I am not driving real fast due to the weather. The job is about five minutes from where we are. We arrive at the scene in six minutes. There is a boy sitting on the steps in front of his house. His foot is wrapped in a towel covered in blood. He is yelling in pain.

"Where is the dog"? I ask.

"I don't know it took off" he replies.

His mother is running up the street yelling and crying. Mike is examining the wound. I am copy down all the information on the report. We dress and bandage the wound before putting him in the bus. This is so it will not bleed too badly in the back of the warm bus. His mother is starting to calm down. The ankle is mulled pretty badly. We tell her we are taking him to Jamaica Hospital since it is a trauma center.

"Hey Cali you can start out for the hospital" Mike tells me.

I start heading down Woodhaven Boulevard toward Jamaica Avenue. I turn right on Jamaica Avenue. And I start to smell something burning in the cab of the bus.

"Are you smoking"? Mike yells.

"Hell no!"

"Where is the smoke coming from"?

"Holly shit it is coming from the dash".

The ambulance comes to stop three buildings from a fire station. I hit the emergency button.

"Four-Three-Adam we have an emergency. Are ambulance is on fire and we have a patient in the back. Could you please send us assistance"?

"Ten-four, Four-Three-Adam will send you help" the dispatcher responds.

We get the patient out of the back of the bus. And we place him inside a deli to stay warm. We use the fire extinguisher on the fire in the dash. But the fire is getting bigger. And the fire extinguisher is little help.

I can hear the sirens coming. All the sudden there is another ambulance on scene for the patient. We place the patient in the back of the second ambulance. Mike gives them a report and a copy of the ambulance call report. The fire now has the cab of the ambulance involved in flames. All the sudden the engine and ladder trucks show up. They put the fire out in a couple of minutes. They are now overhauling the engine compartment and cab of the ambulance. There is not much left. Also a patrol boss is on the scene now taking a report. I saved my backpack, which has a little camera in it.

I take a couple of pictures of the burned out cab. Then I take one of the fire-fighters, Mike, and myself in front of the bus.

"Well you will have to wait for a towtruck to show up. I will take your equipment back to the station" the lieutenant tells us.

"Ok" I reply.

The engine company captain tells us we can wait in the fire station for the towtruck. We now it will be a while. I have waited up to eight hours for a department towtruck to show up. So we might as well be conformable. It takes about six hours for the towtruck to arrive.

"Hey you guys did a good job on this one" the driver tells us.

He hooks the ambulance up to the towtruck and takes off for Maspeth Queens. That is where the Central Repair Facility is located. We call our station from the fire station.

"Station Forty-One Lieutenant Smith"

"Hello Lieutenant Smith this is Cali on Four-Zero-Boy. We had a fire in the ambulance. It is out now and the tow truck has taken it to Maspeth. We are at the fire station on Jamaica Ave. in Richmond Hill. Could you please send some one to pick us up"?

"Ok it will be awhile".

"No problem we will be waiting".

"Hey this is easy overtime" Mike states

"I now" I reply.

We finally get back to the station. It is one in the mourning. That was some of the easiest overtime I have ever done.

Well I have made it through the winter in beautiful Far Rockaway Queens. And yes it dose get very cold down here. The wind cut right through you. Anyway it is spring now and it is starting to get warm out. It is pouring rain out as I make my way to the station. It is a lot better the cold and snow I think to myself. There are large puddles of water everywhere. Since you are at sea level there is no place for the water to go. I get to the station at the usual time. There is Frank waiting for me.

"Hey they put us in a real piece of shit today. Our bus got sent out for preventive maintenance." Frank tells me as I enter the station.

"Great does it leak?"

"Yea at the boot in the cab. I put a towel there to absorb the water" Frank replies.

Oh well it should be an exciting day I think to myself. I get my gear and put it on the truck.

"Hey Cali you're driving today. I do not feel like driving. All I want is a quite Sunday". Frank tells me.

"Ok first stop the deli on Beach 116 street," I say.

"Sounds good to me"

"Ok were out of here".

We start heading to Beach 116 Street. We are starting to hear a squeezing noise in the engine compartment. So I pull into the McDonalds parking lot. All the sudden we hear a bang and there is steam coming out of the engine compartment.

"Holly shit what was that?"

"I don't know".

The truck comes to a stop in a parking place in the lot. We get out and raise the hood. There is steam all over the place.

"Holly shit the water pump went through the radiator".

"Well we are out of service let's go inside McDonalds and call the station".

Frank calls the station on his cell phone. He tells Lieutenant Mitch what happen. You can hear them talking on the phone.

"Hey Lieutenant Mitch you will not believe this but the water pump went through the radiator on the bus".

"Hey Cali they are sending roadside over to check out the bus. We are to wait here. We might as well get something to eat". Frank states.

It is now seven thirty in the mourning.

Well it is now about twelve noon. People are starting to come in for lunch. We are still waiting. We are watching my little television. You can smell them cooking the food. Still no roadside has shown up yet. We are getting board as the time keeps passing by. It is starting to get close to dinnertime finally the mechanic shows up. The mechanic takes a look at the bus.

"Yea I put an order in for a tow truck it should be here within an hour" he tells us.

He gets in his truck and leaves. It is now dinnertime. I am hungry and decide to get a burger. We have now been in the parking lot for nine hours. It is still raining outside. Finally a tow truck arrives. It is seven at night. We have been at McDonalds for twelve hours. He hooks up the bus and drops us off at the station. I think to myself that was an easy four hours of overtime I am tired from sitting around get in my truck and head home.

QUEENS EXPERENCE

Well I have made it through the summer in Far Rockaway. It is August and the weather is starting to get cooler. The humidity is dying down. It is starting to get very conformable. There is usually a nice breeze blowing off the ocean. I am still working up in Howard Beach section of Queens. We are heading up to our area.

When I look and see all this smoke toward Brooklyn.

"Holy shit what's on fire"?

"Don't know let's go check it out" Vinny replies.

We start heading in the direction of the smoke. You can smell smoke as we get closer. Then we see it. It is a major brush fire off of Jamaica Bay. Well it is big for New York City. Since I am from California it is not that big for me.

We get on the radio "Four-three-Adam Queens show us flagged at a brushfire at 156 Ave. and Crossbay in Howard Beech"

"Ten four what's on fire?"

"A large brush fire, fire is on location".

"Queens to Four-Three-Adam they are stating it is two alarms going to three, switch to citywide".

"Ten four switching to citywide".

"Four-three-Adam to citywide".

"Citywide we are sending you a Patrol Boss".

"Ten-four where is staging? 156 Ave and Crossbay potential are to firefighters only, ten-four "Your designation will be Box 5251".

"Ten-four".

I wonder who will be the patrol boss. I think to myself. By now we are starting to setup a treatment and transport area. The fire is burning at a fast rate consuming everything in its path. I start to feel like I am back in California again on the brushfires. As I watch and perform my job I notice that they don't have brush gear. They are using their structural turnout gear. I think to myself they have to be sweating their balls off in the hot weather. It has been about an hour into the fire and about an hour and a half into the shift. There is a helicopter there from New York police Department making water drops on the fire. You can see the fire starting to die down.

But we will be there for a long time. So I start to make myself conformable. So far there has been no injury for which that is a good thing. The Lieutenant is running the job now. We are there just to treat any injured firefighters.

All the sudden a firefighter comes running toward use.

He states "I got burned on the back of my neck".

I look there he has first and second degree burns to the back of the neck. It is still burning he tells us. I start cooling the area with sterile water. My partner starts filling out the paperwork. We will have to transport him to the burn center. The lieutenant tells use to take the firefighter to New York Cornell Burn Center in Manhattan.

You can now see the blisters on his neck starting to form. I have cooled the area and am going to wrap the area in a sterile dressing loosely.

"Hey Cali is you ready to transport".

"Yea I am ready"

We are heading to Manhattan to the burn center. Vinnny is driving he has been on the job about five years. He knows how to get to Manhattan. It will be about a thirty-minute ride. We radio ahead and the dispatcher notifies the hospital. They will be waiting when we arrive.

I can see we are going over the Queensboro Bridge into Manhattan. We will be there in about another five minutes. The patient is still complaining about the pain in his neck from the burn.

I tell him "we will there soon".

"All right" he replies

We pull up the ramp and into the emergency parking area. We pull the stretcher out with the patient and head to the emergency room entrance. The hospital burn team is waiting for use. They start taking the dressing and bandages off. You can see the large blisters on his neck.

He tells "I am in a lot of pain can you give something for the pain".

The doctor states "we will give you something for the pain".

I am giving a report top he nurses. She signs my paperwork. I give her two copies and head back to the bus. Vinny is inside kicking back waiting for me.

"Hey we need to do tracking since it was a member of service".

"Yea I will do it through the Mobil data terminal (MDT)".

"Ok"

I start putting all the information into the computer.

"Hey Cali lets try and stay in Manhattan for a while"

"Yea that sounds good".

There are good looking women all over the place. I am looking at all the women and all the skyscrapers. Vinny starts to head back to Queens.

We are heading down Second Ave towards the Queensboro Bridge. There are good looking women all over the place. I am thinking to myself. I should transfer to Manhattan. But then I start thinking of all the traffic to and from work. Where I am now it only takes me fifteen minutes to get to the station. The next thing I know we are at the bridge heading back into Queens.

We are now in Queens on Queens Blouvard. I ask Vinny to stop at a Seven-Eleven to get a soda. I am very thirsty.

"Hey Vinny do you went anything to drink?"

"Yea get me a Diet Coke.

"All right I got it".

Our tour is just about over. We have about an hour left and it will be time to head back to Rockaway. It has been an exciting night I think to myself. I will be off for the next three days. I will probably go hang out with a couple of friends.

Well it was a nice three days off. Now it is time to go back to work. I now I will be working up in Howard Beach again. It is a pretty nice area to work. You are not that busy. And the people there are nice and easy to get along with. I decide to ride my motorcycle to work today. It is a nice day outside. I will be at the station in about fifteen minutes.

I go in the station.

"Hey Cali, They are putting a new unit in service. It is a tactical unit. You are going to be assigned to it. It is going to be Four-Zero-Boy. It is going to sit up on the mainland near JFK Airport". Frank tells me.

"Cool are you going to be on to be on it"?

"Yea it is going to me you and Oscar Stand".

"Cool Ok when is it going into service"?

"Today the Lieutenant Missel will tell you at roll call".

"Ok I go in the locker room and put on my uniform and grab my equipment".

Roll-call Roll-call the public address calls out. We all head into the lieutenants office. There is Lieutenant Missel behind the desk.

"They are putting a new unit in service today. It will be called Four-Zero-Boy. It will be a tactical unit and will sit at Rockaway Ave and Sutter in Queens. The unit will be manned tour three and tour two. On tour three it will have Frank Barnes, Cali and Oscar Stand. Are there any questions? OK that is all, be safe and have a good tour".

We leave the office and go check out the vehicle we will be in. I have worked with both guys before. They are fun to work with. We should have a good time on the truck. It should be pretty busy. This is because it sits in a rough area of Southern Queens. We start heading up to the mainland. I am driving and Frank is the technician today. It will take use about thirty minutes to get there. We get there I open the map to the area it is new to me.

All the sudden the radio calls out "Four-Zero-Boy switch to Citywide".

"Ten-Four, Four-Zero-Boy to Citywide".

"Four-Zero-Boy I am sending you to the fire in Manhattan at 123rd and Second Ave. It has gone to five alarms, approxmently sixty injuried, staging is at 123rd and First Ave. Conditions Ten is the supervisor in charge".

"Ten-four"

We hit the sixty-three buttons and start responding. It will take use at least thirty minutes to get there. We look on the map it looks like the Tri-Bourgh Bridge is the best way to enter the area.

As we are responding I am thinking we are going to be there for a while. This must be a really bad fire. It is a five-story apartment building fully involved in fire. I now we will be working hard for a while. I turn the map page to the area we are responding to. Frank is looking up information on the computer as we are responding. We arrive at the scene in about thirty minutes. We see the staging officer.

"You guys report to transportation area. Back your bus in over there where the busses and parked. You guys will receive patients from the treatment area".

"Yes sir".

"Do you know where the hospitals area located in Manhattan?"

"No sir we are a Queens Tactical unit".

"Ok you have a map correct".

"Yes sir".

"Ok we will give you the address and directions to the hospital".

Most of the patients are walking wounded. Mainly smoke inhalation. So stand by you bus. Go ahead and leave your bus running. There are ten other ambulances here with us in the staging area. There are a total of sixteen ambulances and three lieutenants on scene. This is our first MCI (mass causality incident). I am surprise at how calmly it is being handled. I guess in New York this is no big deal.

"Four-Zero-Boy I have four patients for you. They are walking wounded. Transport them to Metropolitan Hospital that is hospital ten. It is located at Nine-three Street and Second Ave. in Manhattan".

"Ok sir".

I look up the location of the hospital on the map. Frank is loading the patients in the back of the bus. I assist Frank with filling out the Ambulance Call Reports. It is about twenty blocks away, and should take use about ten minutes to get there. We start out for the hospital and we get there in about eight minutes.

We take the patients into the emergency room to be triage.

"What do you guys have"? A nurse asks.

"We have four patients from the fire to be checked out".

"Ok take then out to the triage area. The triage nurse will sign for them".

We take them out to the waiting area. It is packed with patients. Frank talks to the triage nurse she signs for all the patients. It is about three hours in to our shift now. We start heading back out to the bus.

"Four-Zero-Boy to Citywide head back to the fire".

"Negative Four-Zero-Boy head back to Queens. You have been released from the fire thanks for your help".

We switch back to the Queens frequency

"I hope we can get back to Queens before we get another job" I say to Frank.

"Yea no shit" he replies

As we head back to the TriBourgh Bridge. We should be back in Queens in about fifteen minutes.

We get back in Queens.

"Hey Cali stop I what to get something to drink".

I pull into a deli.

"You what anything"?

"Shore I will take a Diet coke".

"Ok got it".

We start heading back to our area. The radio is quite. Not much going on in Queens at present. We get back to our area in about another fifteen minutes. The rest of the shift goes by with no jobs. We get back to the station.

"Hey Cali you have training orders hear. You are going to refresher at the academy for three weeks. Here sign for them" the lieutenant tells me.

I think to myself three weeks off the street. What a nice vacation. I get the weekend off and then report to the academy.

Refresher is not bad. It is three weeks of reviewing all the skills you need to be an Emergency Medical Technician. You go to refresher every three years. It can be a lot of fun. You meet people that were in your original class. I will take my motorcycle to refresher. This is because there is no parking. There are about thirty of use in the class. I now five people in the class. I have not seen them in a year.

Well I get to the academy a little early. Find a place to park. Here comes Pete in one of my old partners from Coney Island.

"Hey where are you at now"? He asks

"I am at Far rockaway station forty-one".

"That's cool".

"Yea it's alright I knida miss Coney though". I reply.

"You ready for refresher?"

"Yea as ready as I will ever bee".

"Ok let's go then".

We take off walking up the hill from the jetty.

We enter the academy and find out what classroom we are in. The first week and half is all academic. Instructor Reading goes over different treatment and rules. Discussing anything knew that the state is proposing that we will be performing in the field. There is really nothing new. I try not to fall asleep during the lecture.

We are in the second part of refresher. This is where we have to perform all our skills for the instructors. So they give us couple of days to practice before they test use. The next thing I know it is time for skills testing. I perform all my skills. They tell me I passed the skills session. And my state written test will be tomorrow night. All you have to do is come in take the written test. Then you can leave. That will be cool then I can go hang out.

I take the written test. It is not that hard. There are one hundred questions. And most of them are common sense. I get a letter in the mail in about a week with my new card. It is good for another three years. It was a nice three weeks of the street. But I did miss working the streets. You get a lot of different type of calls in the street. It is never a dual.

I am taking a couple of days off work to help a friend out down in Pennsylvania. It is where I lived as a teenager. I am going to deliver some kind of mail for him from New York. He has a courier business. And dose not now the area that well.

I am driving his truck along Route One in Avondale Pa. When I see a car hit an oil tank truck head-on. The driver of the car is trapped in the driversseat. By the steeringwheel and the dash is wrapped around him. I pull my truck to the side of the road. Jump out and see if I can help him. Other cars are pulling over to assist. The driver of the oil truck jumps out.

"Are you ok"? I ask.

"Yes" he replies.

He tells me I called the accident in. Help is on the way. Ok thanks. The next thing I see is a police officer pulling over.

I tell him "My name is James Thompson I work for New York City Emergency Medical Service. I need a helicopter and rescue for the driver of the car. The oil truck is leaking heating oil".

The police officer goes to his car calls in the information. He then gives me a first-aid kit from the car. There is not much equipment in it for the patient. He can see that he has a flail chest and difficulty in breathing. I am hearing more sirens coming. I hope this is the fire department. I have been on the scene for about five minutes now. Fire equipment is starting to pull up. There is a paramedic unit arriving on scene. All the sudden I hear the helicopter coming into land.

I give the paramedics my report on the patient. They agree with me on the treatment. By this time the rescue team has removed the patient from the wreckage. And they are preparing him transport to the trauma center in the helicopter. The officer asks me for my information for the police report. I give him all the information.

I continue on my way making my last delivery. I head back up to New York. I am back in the station now. Not much is going on. I have all but forgotten about the job down in Pennsylvania. There have been no exciting jobs. It has been a week since I was in Pennsylvania. The station lieutenant tells me he has a letter for me. It is from headquarters. I wonder what it is. It is a certificate of apperception from Chester County Pennsylvania for stopping at the accident.

There is also a letter with it. It says thank you for stopping. But do the injuries the patient had he did not make it. He died at the trauma center.

The Lieutenant tells me "Good job"

"Thanks"

A couple of guys at the station want to see the letter. I go ahead and show it to them. Not much has been going on for the last couple weeks. We have been responding to the regular jobs. I am sick; my stomach hurts that kind of thing. And of course the good old I have fallen and can't get up.

I get to the station today. There is a notice up on the wall. It states they have openings in Special Operations Division. I think great. I have wanted to get into Special Operations since coming on the job. I read all the requirements. And I find out that I meet all the requirements.

I call down to Special Operations.

"Yes this is James Thompson I would like to take the test for SOD"

"No problem we will notify of you when the test will be given. It will consist of general EMT nonlegence and the operations guide. You should now the emergency action plan". The lieutenant tells me over the phone.

I get to the station and park my truck. As I am walking up the apron to the station, I felt something on my right arm. The next thing I feel is sharp pain and I can't breathe. Oh shit I have been stung by a bee. I am highly allergic to bees. As I fall to the ground I grab my epipen and jab my thigh. Lt Keefe comes running out to me.

"What's wrong Thompson he yells"?

"Beesting Beesting I can feel my throat closing up".

"Hey Pete call for medics Thompson been stung by a bee. He is having an allergic reaction. Get me the spare medic bag". He yells

He starts to treat me with the medication I need. I am still having trouble breathing. I am just barely able to move air in and out of my lungs. They start bagging me with force ventilation. Lieutenant Keefe signs me on duty so it will be a line of duty incident.

The medics arrive also the duty captain arrives. They place on the stretcher and take off for the hospital. I am breathing a little better now. But I still cannot talk. They wheel into the emergency room. I know all the nurse there and doctor. Because this is the hospital we bring most of the patients to. The chief has called ahead so they are expecting me. After about an hour I am starting to fell better. All the drugs have taken effect. At least I will not have to be amitted to the hospital this time.

I start thinking to myself. Maybe I should have stayed in California. There are hardly any bees in Las Angeles due to the smog. I have been stung twice since I have been in New York. Different crews are stopping and seeing how I am doing which makes me feel good. They tell me call the station when I am discharged and someone will pick me up.

I call the station.

"Hello this is Cali can somebody come pick me up. They are discharging me".

"Ok I will send the patrol boss down. He should be there in a couple of minutes".

The patrol boss shows up.

"Cali you have to fill out the incident report". Ok "How many days did they put you off work"?

"They put me out for the next three days"

"Ok we will take you off the schulde. It will be line of duty injury." He tells me.

We head back to the station. My chest is still painful from sting as I head back to the station. I get ready and head home for a couple of days of relaxation.

"Four-Zero-Boy for the stab at Sutter and Basely Street".

It is about five blocks from where we are sit. We turn on the lights and head to the location.

"I wonder where he got cut"?

"Don't Know Frank replies".

We pull up to the corner. There is a group of people waving to use and yelling hurry up. There we find a patient about twenty with his throat slashed. You can see the blood pumping out of the wound. The carotid artery has been cut.

I am teching. We garb the patient put him on the streatcher. I start apply pressure to wound to control the bleeding. Frank is driving.

"OK lets get out here call hospital 36 tell them we got a twenty year old with a cut carotid artery uncontrollable bleeding"

"You ready for me to leave?"

"Yea get rolling".

We take off for the hospital. Frank is hauling balls. It will be about a five-minute ride. The back of the ambulance is bouncing around as Frank goes down the streets. I cannot get a blood pressure on the patient and his pulse is real week. His breathing is real shallow also try and bag him the best I can. I have to also hold pressure on the wound. This guy is in bad shape.

We turn the corner I can see we are one block from the trauma center. As we back to the doors there is another crew there to help use out. I am still holding pressure on the wound. They grab the stretcher.

"OK I ready when you guys are. Somebody is going to have bag him".

Another crewmember grabs the mask and starts bagging the patient as we head to the trauma room. They are waiting for se in the room.

"We don't have much information on him. Twenty-year-old cut to the neck with a razor blade. They got the catroid artery." I tell the trauma room staff.

The trauma team starts getting the patient stabilized. The back of the bus is a mess. There is blood all over thee place. We will be out of service for a while cleaning it up. Frank starts cleaning up the back of the bus. The police have arrived and have information on the patient. I start filling out the ambulance call report. There is too much for use to clean so we decide to go back to the station and clean the bus. Plus it is getting close to the end of shift.

"Four-Zero-Boy put use out Blood Bourne Pathogens".

"Ten-four Four-Zero-Boy".

"Frank that was a hell of job we had'.

"No shit lets get something to drink for the ride back to the station'.

"Ok".

We get back to the station in about thirty minutes. It will take use another thirty minutes to clean the back of the ambulance. Everything has blood all over it.

It is a Saturday. I am just getting off working the night tour. When we hear a job go out for a train wreck on the Williamsburg Bridge.

The desk Lieutenant tells me "Grab the Mass Causality Incident van and head towards the bridge".

"OK sir".

This is a small van we have that carries extra backboard collars and other equipment. This is a Manhattan bound train. So there would be a lot of people on it. It will take me about thirty minutes to get there.

I get there there is emergency equipment all over the place. I find the Incident Commander.

"Sir Thompson from Station Forty-one. I have the MCI van with me where do you want me"?

"Go to the treatment area and help set up".

There are a lot of patients complaining of neck and back pain. They will all have to be boarded and collared.

I start passing out equipment to other medical personal in the treatment area. The next thing I notice my van is empty of boards. I have given out fifty backboards. I tell the treatment officer.

"I am out of boards what do you want me to do"?

"Just copy down a list of what all supplies you used and give it to me".

The incident has been going on for about thirty minutes now. All the patients have been triaged and are getting ready to be transported to area hospitals. There are a total of sixty-four patients to be transported to the hospital. The job has taken one hour from start to finish. I will start heading to the hospitals to collect boards. This way I can restock the unit and place it back in service. It is easy over-time for a Saturday morning.

BLIZZARD OF 1996

Well it is starting to get cold out. Thanksgiving has come and gone. You can feel the cold air blowing off the ocean. We are wearing are winter uniforms. They are talking about the bad weather on the news. I hope it is not too bad. I don't like snow and the cold. I guess you could say New York is the wrong place for me. But I am back here now and will have to deal with it. Christmas is just around the corner. There have been the usual jobs nothing exciting. I am working Christmas day but will be off New Years and plan to go to Time Square.

It is Christmas day I am working tour three the afternoon shift. We have just eaten turkey dinner at the station. All the sudden the radio gives us a job.

"Four-One-Eddie for the stabbing at 839 Beach 241 Street apartment 88 David" the dispatcher calls out.

"Ten-four responding"

I am working with Rob Front. We hit the sixty-three button. It is only about five minutes from the station. We are on the scene within four minutes. Police are there and telling us to hurry up.

We rush into the apartment. There is an elderly lady on the floor with a knife in her chest. I check her breathing she is in respiratory arrest. I then feel for a pulse it is absent. I roll her on her back and start resuscitation measures on her.

"Rob call for medics we got an arrest," I yell.

"Four-One-Eddie we need medics for a traumatic arrest," Rob yells into the radio.

"Ten-four, Four-One-Young is responding" the dispatcher states.

They get here in about three minutes. Still there are no signs of life. They start performing advance life support on her. They have made the decision to transport her to the hospital two minutes away. Not a trauma center due to she is in arrest. We have all the information on her a cop tells us.

"Is she likely"? The cop asks.

"Yes she is in arrest" I reply.

We head to the ambulance. We are working on her all the way down in the elevator. It is tight and we are doing the best we can.

"Four-One-Eddie with a notification to hospital thirty-seven.
"Four-One-Eddie go ahead" the dispatcher replies.

"Notify hospital thirty-seven we are in bound with sixty year old female. Traumatic arrest, knife in the chest".

"Ten-four they are waiting for you" she replies.

We arrive at the hospital in about three minutes. I back the ambulance up to the entrance. The emergency room team is waiting for us.

We wheel the patient into the treatment room. The doctor starts giving orders. They are in there working on her for a couple minutes. Then comes out and tells us.

"She was stabbed through the heart, she never had a chance".

I think to myself there goes my Christmas cheer. The police are at the hospital now.

"Did she make it"? The cop asks.

"No she was stabbed through the heart" the doctor responds.

"The daughter got mad because her brother got a bigger piece of meat. She then grabbed a steak knife and stabbed her mother in the chest. She is now under arrest". The cop tells us.

I think to myself how can people live like that. How can you have so much hate for your parents to do something like that? But you see it a lot in the city. It gets to a point you do not think about it anymore.

Well it is New Years Eve a couple of my friends have meant me. We are going to Time Square to watch the ball fall. It should be fun. I have called the officer at Station Eleven to see if I can park my truck there. He said I could then we will take to the train to Time Square. This should be real exciting I have never been there before. It was real cold and I hate the cold. But it was worth it.

It is now January 1996. The news and the weather station keep saying. We are going to have a major blizzard this month. I hope it does not come true. All the sudden it is cold and the snow starts coming down. It is snowing and blowing cold air. I get in my truck warm it up and drive to the station. It is not bad driving. I have four wheel drive and can go basically anywhere. The snow is about a foot deep and drifting across the road. It takes me about thirty minutes to get to the station. I park and go inside.

"Roll call, roll call" Lieutenant Missel calls out over the public address system.

We head into the supervisor's office.

"Ok guys as you can see it is snowing outside. According to weather reports we are to get thirty-six inches of snow. And operations have issued an order. We are going to be working sixteen-hour shifts for the next couple of days. So be safe out there and stay dry. That is all" he states.

We exit the office and head toward the ambulances to put our equipment on them.

"Hey Cali do you want to drive"?

"Yes shore this should be interesting" I reply.

We check out the ambulance and head toward the mainland. It takes us about thirty minutes to get to our area. Rob is reading a book. I am reading the newspaper. All the sudden the radio calls out.

"Four-Zero-Boy head back to the Rock they are going into back log with jobs" the dispatcher tells us.

"Ten-four heading back to the Rock" I reply.

That means there are more jobs then the units available. And those jobs are holding in the communications center. And there are no ambulances to dispatch for that area of the city.

We start heading back. You can hardly see the road it is snowing really badly.

"Let's take the Van Wyck and the back way in to Rockaway. It should be better then going through Broad Channel" Bob tells me.

"Ok" I reply.

I start heading toward the Van Wyck Expressway. We are going down Foch Street. There are cars slipping and sliding all over the place. One car slid through a stop sign and hit almost hit us.

"Oh shit the windshield wipers are starting to freeze up" I yell.

I pull over get out and hit the wipers against the glass. The ice breaks off. It has taken us fifteen minutes to go what should have taken us five minutes. We are now about three blocks from the Van Wcyk. It looks like a giant parking lot. There are cars slipping and sliding all over the place. There are vehicles stuck in the snow. And no one is moving.

"Hey Rob I think we should try and go through Broad Channel we are going to be stuck here for a while".

"Go for it you are driving" Bob replies.

We turn around and start heading toward Crossbay Boulevard. We head down Foch to Rockaway Avenue. Rockaway Avenue is a main street and seams to be in better condition. We are able to get behind a Department of Sanitation snowplow. We will let him clear the road for us.

"Four-Zero-Boy what is your estimated time to the Rock"? The dispatcher asks.

"We are heading toward the Rock. We are on Crossbay Boulevard now. We are behind a snowplow." Bob replies over the radio.

"Ten-four try and get down as soon as you can" the dispatcher replies.

We finally get to Crossbay Boulevard. It has been plowed.

"Hey this is not bad we should be able to get to the bridge without a problem," I say

It has been snowing all day. There is about two feet of snow on the ground. And of course people are driving and walking in it. We are start heading down Crossbay the road is clear. It takes us twenty minutes to get to the first bridge into Broad Channel. This is a small island in Queens connected by two bridges. It generally floods pretty bad when it rains, and is not much better in the snow. There are cars parked all over the place in Broad Channel. We are able to get through Broad Channel without a problem. We cross the second bridge and now are in the Rockaways. The whole trip has taken us about an hour.

"Four-Zero-Boy Queens we are in the Rock and available" Rob tells the dispatcher.

"Ten-four I have a job for you. The sick at Two Two One Beach Nine Zero Street. It has been holding for a while". The dispatcher replies.

"Ten-four got it" Rob replies.

The address is just across from the bridge. We pull up in front of the house in a couple minutes. I get out and grab the chair. Rob grabs his equipment. We climb over the snow bank from the snowplows to get to the house. I climb up the steps onto the porch and ring the doorbell. The door opens and an elderly lady opens the doors.

She says "My husband does not feel good can you take him to the hospital. I would like him to go to Peninsula Hospital".

"No problem" I reply.

We enter the house there stuff everywhere. We finally get to the couch. There is an elderly man laying on it. He is sweating and pale. It looks like a cardiac.

"He states "My chest hurts a lot".

I start getting all the information and filling out the report. Bob is interview the patient and taking his vital signs.

"Hey Cali call for medics" Rob tells me.

"Four-Zero-Boy request medics for a cardiac"

"Four-Zero-Boy no medics available at this time package and transport" the dispatcher tells us.

We have the patient on oxygen and place him in the chair. He is not a big person thank goodness.

"Hey I will take all the equipment out to the bus and open the back doors" I tell Rob.

I grab all the equipment and head back out to the ambulance. Back over the snow piles to the back of the ambulance, which now the snow has piled up against. I kick the snow away from the back doors and finally get them open. And put all the equipment inside and turn on the heat. I leave them cracked open and head back through the snow and in to the house.

Rob has the patient secured to the chair and covered with a blanket.

"Ok sir we are taking you out to the bus. Do not grab on to anything. And we have the heat on in the back" I tell the patient.

We start to carry him down the stairs. We are making sure not to slip. Then it is over the snow banks to the ambulance. It takes us about ten minutes to get him in the back. Then I go back and get his wife. She is scared she is going to fall in the snow.

I tell her "I will not let you fall just hold on".

She does and we finally get to the bus. This has taken us a total of fifteen minutes. It fells good to be back in the warm ambulance.

It will take us about fifteen minutes to get to the hospital. The snow is still coming down as we head to the hospital. It is a blinding snow. You can hardly see where you are going. I have to negotiate around cars stuck in the snow and people walking in the street. It takes us ten minutes to get to the hospital.

I tell "Mrs. Smith wait for me, we are going to take your husband inside. Then I will come back out and get you".

I go to the back and meet Rob. We unload the patient and take him into the emergency room. It feels good to be inside where it is warm and dry.

Rob is giving the report to the emergency room nurse. I wheel the stretcher over to the hospital stretcher. Bob joins me and we the patient over to the stretcher. Rob goes back and nurse has signed for the patient. I am making up the stretcher wishing I could stay inside and keep warm and dry. I still have eight more hours to go. It will be a long and cold night.

It is now around two in the mourning. The snow is starting to diminish. We have gotten a total of thirty-eight inches of snow. We have been informed by the radio that we are in a snow emergency. And that the National Guard has been called in to assist us with Hummer Ambulances. I think to myself that we can us the help. We leave the hospital and go available.

"Four-Zero-Boy for the abdominal pain at 234 Seaport Beachcrest apartment 25David on the twenty-fifth floor. You have a fifteen year old female with a stomach ache" the dispatcher tells us.

"Four-Zero-Boy ten four sixty-three"

It is about thirty blocks from where we are. Seaport is a main road and should be clear of snow. I hit the sixty-three button and start responding to the call. The main roads are snow covered. But they are passable.

"Hey Cali do you now what sanitation call this white gold. They are all over-time clearing the streets" Bob tells me.

I think that maybe I should go to work for sanitation. We are getting close to the apartment complex now. There are snow piles on both sides of the road.

"Oh shit" I yell.

The ambulance slides on the ice and into a snow pile at the entrance to the apartment complex.

"I think we are stuck," I say

"Yea we are" Rob replies.

I put the ambulance in reverse and try and back out. Nothing happens, I look there is snow up to the windows. We cannot even open the doors to get out. So we roll down the windows and climb out through them. It is cold and wet out-side.

"Four-Zero-Boy to Queens"

"Queens go ahead"

"Four-Zero-Boy we are stuck in the snow in front of Beachcrest on Seaport Boulevard," I say.

"Ten-four will send a patrol boss"

We hear the dispatcher tell Four-On Patrol to respond to us. That we are stuck in the snow in front of the apartment complex. I get my camera out and take a couple of pictures. All you can see is the top half of the ambulance. The rest is buried in the snow. A couple of minute's pass and we hear this noise. It is one of the ambulance Hummers. It comes down the street and through the snow bank like it is not even there. It takes the patrol boss about thirty minutes to get to us. As he pulls up the Hummer comes out of the complex and through the snow on its way to the hospital.

Lieutenant Daz is the patrol boss. He is a pretty lay back type of boss. His first question to us was.

"How did you do this"?

"It was easy sir we hit the ice and this is where we landed" I reply.

"Ok here is the chain, get under the bumper and hook it to the frame. I will try and pull you out"

I craw under the bumper and hook the chain to the frame. He gets in his vehicle and pulls the chain tight. He then tries to pull the ambulance out of the snow bank. He makes three attempts and nothing happens.

"You guys are really stuck. Let me see if sanitation will come down and get you guys out" he tells us.

He takes off for the sanitation garage. It is near our station. It will take him at least forty-five minutes till he returns. We have clear the snow away from the exhaust pipe so we can sit inside and stay warm. Lieutenant Daz returns in an hour.

"I have sanitation coming down with one of there tow trucks. They should be here soon. You guys wait in my vehicle. Hear have some hot chocolate"

The big tow truck shows up thirty minutes after the lieutenant.

"Hey you guys did a real good job of getting stuck" he replies.

"Thanks"

Hey grabs the hooks off the truck, and hooks up to the ambulance. He checks to make sure it is in neutral. He starts to pull the ambulance. It does not move at first. You can see the tension on the cables. Then he pulls again a little harder. Still it does not move. We are sitting in the patrol vehicle in case the cables break. He tries for the third time. You can hear the tension on the cables now. They are very tight. The ambulance is starting to move. You can hear the trucks engine. Finally the ambulance is free from the snow bank. It is almost six in the mourning. Our shift will over in about an hour.

We tell the tow truck operator thanks. We offer to get him some hot chocolate but he takes off. We get back in the ambulance and start heading back to the station. We should be there in thirty minutes. The sun is starting to come up. We get back and it is time to get ready to go home. I will be home only for six hours. Then it will be back to the station. We will be working this schedule for about a week.

I get back to the station. It feels like I never left. Chief Pek is signaling me into the office.

"What happened last shift"? He ask

"I got stuck in the snow sir" I reply.

"I heard, well I am assigning you to the Hummers. I cannot afford to pay you to be stuck in the snow. Good luck be safe"

"Yes sir"

Well at least I will be in the station where it is warm and dry. I have brought my old fire department turn out gear with me. It will keep me warm and dry when I am out in the field. And the officers are not busting balls on what you are wearing. There are guys wearing snow skiing suits. They are just glad you are showing up for work.

They have assigned the Hummers seven-one numbers. They are still using the same letters to state weather you are basic life support or advance life support. We are assigned the call sign Seven-One-Alpha. This means we are a Hummer ambulance basic life support. I go over and meet the two National Guard Medics. They are there to drive. Rob and I will be the two emergency medical technicians on the unit.

"Seven-One-Alpha for the OB. You have a labor at 4225 Beach 31 Street private house. Patient is nine months pregnant and contractions are two minutes apart" the dispatcher tells us.

"Ten-four sixty-three" I reply

We take off for the job. Since there are no lights and sirens it will take us longer to get there. The call is about thirty blocks from the station. We get there in about ten minutes.

"Seven-One-Alpha eighty-eight:"

There is a guy out front flagging us down.

"Hurry man she is having a baby" he yells.

I grab my tech bag and head into the house. There is a lady on the couch. You can tell she is in pain.

"Has your water broken"?

"Yes about ten minutes ago"

"Is this your first child, are there any complications"?

"No complication, I have four other children all normal births".

"Ok we will put you in the chair and take you over to the hospital"

We put her in the chair and carry her to the ambulance. She is in the back in a couple of minutes. It will be easier to deliver there then in the house. You can hear her scream with the labor pains.

The two National Guardsman jump in the back. They now how to use all the equipment in the back.

"The baby is coming," she yells

"Ok"

I take a look you can see the head coming out and going back in.

"Hey Rob get ready for a delivery" I tell him.

"Ok"

We will deliver on the stretcher. She yells again this time the head is starting to appear. There is blood all over the place. I place my hand on the head and start to guide it out. Then I guide the rest of the baby out. We suction the mouth and nose. It takes about five minutes to deliver the baby. The baby and the mother are doing fine. One of the guardsmen looks a little pale. The other one climb up front when she started to deliver.

We take off or the hospital. Rob tells the dispatcher what is going on and we are going to the hospital. It will take us a couple of minutes to get to the hospital. The guardsman tells us this is the first time he has ever seen a baby delivered. He them vomits in the back. We tell him to go sit up front.

We head back to the station to clean up the back of the Hummer. It takes us a while to clean up all equipment. It was a pretty interesting call. The guardsmen are felling better now. And he looks better. The rest of the shift is not that eventful. And another sixteen-hour shift has passed. We will be doing this for the next five days. It seam as soon as you get home it is time to come back to work. Well the snow emergency is starting to wine down. They have released the Hummers and we are going back to eight-hour shifts. I made a fair amount of overtime during the storm. And will spend a good part of it on a nice vacation in of course southern California. The rest of the winter is not that bad. A couple of small snow storms. I will be glad when spring arrives.

THE MERGER

"Hey Cali we got a new lieutenant in the station. This guy is by the book. He is from Manhattan" Greg tells me.

"Great just what we need down here. What is his name?"

"Lieutenant Klump"

"Ok I now who he is. I saw him once in Manhattan. He lives in Long Beach" I reply.

Well it is getting close to the big merger of the New York City Emergency Medical Service into the Fire Department City of New York or FDNY for short. There are a lot of rumors flying around. The biggest one is we are all going to get laid off. Me I am the type of person I need to see it in black and white and signed to believe it. Lieutenant Klump has made a suggestion that we have a death to EMS party at the station. The cake will look like a casket and have EMS on it. And the date will be March 17 1996. Lieutenant Missel is selling tee shirts that say The Best Are Laid To Rest. It is a real lively time at the station.

A couple of firefighters have written in the Chief a newspaper how wrong it is to sell the tee shirts. Also a couple of EMS personnel have written in the paper how bad the merger will be. I am just going with the flow. The job conditions cannot get any worse then they are now. The morale is very low and people are forcing them selves to come to work. I guess it is the not knowing about the job that has people real upset.

I come into the station. And I see the list of all the names of personal transferred to the fire department is up on the board. I go over and read the list names. There I see my name. I have been transferred to the fire department. I think to myself this should be interesting. After all the fire department is only interested in putting out fires. They could care less about responding to medical and trauma emergencies. The firefighters hate us. And most EMS personal dislikes them also.

"Roll Call Roll Call" the desk lieutenant calls out.

"Cali you are working with Frank Domingo today on Four-One-Adam".

"Ok sir"

I have worked with Frank before. He has about ten years on the job and is fun to work with. He is a very relaxed type of partner.

"Hey Cali are you ready to go. I checked out the bus," he yells to me.

"Sure let's hit the beach"

It is starting to get warm. And the women are laying out getting there sun tans. What a nice view for the shift.

We head down to the boardwalk. You can drive on this part. It is concrete. The wood part, the ambulance is too heavy and would fall through. We head over the where you drive up. There are some good-looking females out on the beach. We park the bus and start scanning the beach. All the sudden a patrol supervisor pulls next to us.

"Hey what are you guys doing on the boardwalk"? Lieutenant Klump asks.

"We are not on the boardwalk this is concrete under us" Frank replies.

"We will have to see about that. I will have to talk to the captain".

"Ok what ever".

We talk for a little while then pull away. The rest of the shift is uneventful. I think to myself that this guy is really a dick. He is paper happy like everybody says. I always try and give a person a chance. And not allow other peoples opinion to judge somebody. It is going to be along summer down here with him here. We will not have any fun at Station Forty-One when he is on duty. Maybe he will get board and transfer to another station. I think to myself.

Well summer has started. Oscar is finishing up his nursing school and will be leaving the unit soon. Frank and I are wondering who are new partner will be. It is Frank last shift on. They he will be off for the next couple of days.

"Hey Cali as soon as you find out who are new partner is give me a call," he asks as he leaves the station.

"No problem"

I come into the station. There is a good-looking Italian girl there. She is new and I have never seen her before.

"Hey Cali this is your new partner. Her name is Ginger Mann" Lieutenant Missel tells me.

"Ok" I reply.

I think to myself great a woman just what I need. I wonder if she can lift the patients into the back of the bus. And on top of that she is new to the job. I do not like working with new people. You have to keep an eye on them all the time.

We head out to the ambulance. Ginger starts checking out the vehicle. You can tell she is new. She counts everything and dose a real through check out of the vehicle. She tells me she cannot drive. That she has not been to the Emergency Vehicle Operations Course yet. No problem we are talking about a lot of different things. She seams like she will be a lot of fun to work with.

"I have to call Frank are other partner on the bus".

"Ok what are you going to tell him"? She asks.

"What do you want me to tell him"?

"Tell him that I am a fat, lazy, bitch. That I worked in communication and I hate the job" she replies.

"Ok you got it".

"Hello Frank you should see our new partner"

"Yea, what is she like"

"She is a fat, ugly and hates the job. She worked in communications and is a miserable bitch it seems like."

"All shit we have to put up with this" he replies.

"Yea"

In the mean time Ginger and I are trying hard not to laugh. Frank is taking everything very seriously. I hang up the phone. We start laughing about what I told him.

We head up to the mainland of Queens. It takes us about fifteen minutes to get there. We are talking all the time. Finding out all sorts of information on each other. Then we start joking and laughing about different things. She is going to be a lot of fun to work with. We get a couple of minor bullshit jobs. Nothing to talk about really. Just good old New York City taxi runs. Sometimes you pull up and find a taxi pulling up to the same address. They will take the ambulance they think it is faster. And they use Medicaid so they will not have to pay the bill. We head back to the station. I am off for the next couple of days. Frank will be shocked when he comes into the station. I changed into my jeans, jump on my Ninja and head home.

It is about five in the afternoon. All the sudden my phone rings at the house.

"Hello"

"You are an asshole Cali. I was wondering all night how to get Ginger off the unit" Frank yells at me.

Of course I new Frank would call after he met her. And new he would yell at me. Otherwise it would not be Frank.

"I could not help my self. Anyway she told me what to say".

"Sure she did, I will pay back for this. I have to go we have a job to go to".

"Ok later be safe".

I have been working with Ginger for about a month now. She is a good part-ner and a lot of fun to work with. All three of us are having a good time on the unit.

I enter the station. Lieutenant Missel is on the desk. He is looking at some-thing and shaking his head. I wonder what it is.

"Hey Cali come in the office" he calls to me

"Yes sir"

"Here look at Ginger's Unit Activity Log, She is writing a short story on each job. Do me a favor and show her how to fill it out."

I look over the log. She is writing way too much in the log. It is like each job is a short story. I will talk to her and show her the way it is suppose to be. Short and to the point. I will talk to her when she comes back on shift tomorrow. She is off today and I am extra.

I head into the station. There is Ginger waiting for me. This should be an interesting day. We check out the unit. I go over how to do the Unit Activity Log with her. It takes a couple minutes and she understands what they want. We head up to the mainland. All the sudden the radio calls out.

"Four-Zero-Boy for the drug".

"Four-Zero-Boy give it up"

"You have a heroin overdose at 230 Beach 19 Street cross Street Seaport Blvd. In the rock no medics available" the dispatcher tells us.

We head to the call. Ginger is copy down the information on the report. I am driving; it will take us about fifteen minutes to get there. We are making good time. Traffic is moving for us. We get there in about ten minutes. There is an engine company on scene. They are using a bag valve mask to force oxygen into the patient. It is Jane on of our regular overdose patients. When a person uses heroin, it slows down the breathing and sometimes the patients go into respiratory arrest and then cardiac arrest.

Ginger yells, "There is smoke coming from the right front wheel of the ambulance".

"Oh shit"

I call "Queens Four-Zero-Boy we need medics' respiratory arrest and we are out mechanical"

"Ten-four"

"Four-Zero-Boy medics are twenty minutes out and the closes unit I have is fifteen minutes out" the dispatcher tells us.

"Start them out"

"Ten-four"

I look at the engine company captain. He has two firefighters with fire extinguishers at the bus. He heard the radio message.

"Listen she needs to get to the hospital right away. The hospital is only two blocks from here." he states.

"Yes sir".

"Ok this is what we are going to do. Get the patient in the back of the bus. I will put a firefighter in the back with your partner. I will put a second firefighter up front with you. He will have a fire extinguisher. The engine will escort you to the hospital" he tells me.

Since we are part of the fire department now. Anything that goes wrong the captain will have to explain. I say to myself.

"I will take full responsibility for the decision" he states

"Yes sir"

We start loading the patient in the back of the bus. Everybody is ready we take off for the hospital. We get there in a couple of minutes. We arrive at the hospital with no new problems. The firefighter and Ginger take the patient into the emergency room. I wait at the bus. There is a patrol boss responding to the hospital. I cancel the other units responding to help us.

The patrol boss arrives at the hospital. I tell him what happen. There is still some smoke coming form the right front wheel well. The Engine Company is still there. Finally the smoke dissipates. The patrol boss takes me to the station to get another unit. I tell Ginger what is going on and that I will be back. I arrive at the hospital. There is Ginger outside smoking one cigarette after another.

"Is it always like this down here? I need to transfer to the mainland" she replies

"Yes this is normal for the Rockaways. You see when the shit hits the fan we are all alone down here. And help is about fifteen minutes out" I reply.

We are just about done for the day now. Ginger has started to relax some. I hope the rest of the day will be uneventful. It is now about fourteen thirty hours. As we head back to the station for shift change. We stop at the store I pick up at Diet Coke and a soda for her. That is the least I can do after the day we had. It has been a stressful one. I head home thinking about what all happen today. It is a nice fifteen-minute ride to my apartment. Once home I decide to take a long ride out the Ocean Parkway.

It is time to go back to work. It was a short three days off. I head into the station. Today I am detailed to another unit that is assigned to the Rockaways. I am working with Keith Moon.

"Four-One-Echo for the OB"

"Four-One-Echo give it up"

"You have an OB out at 1234 Beach 44 in the basement and Seaport Blvd."
The dispatcher tells us.

"Ten-four responding"

I am copy down all the information off the computer screen. Keith is driving.
We will be there in a couple minutes. We arrive and can hear people yelling in
the apartment. We enter the apartment. There is a lady on the couch getting
ready to deliver. I pull out the kit and equipment out of my tech bag.

"Its coming" the patient is yelling.

"Look," yells her sister.

The baby is starting to come out. I am delivering the baby. We notice the
baby is limp. The baby appears to be in cardiac arrest.

"Four-One-Echo we need medics newborn in cardiac arrest," Keith yells into
the radio.

"Ten-four sending you a medic unit" the dispatcher tells us.

The baby delivers. We suction and start resuscitation efforts on the baby.
Everybody is crying and yelling. We hear the sirens of additional unit on the way.
Keith takes the baby out of the apartment to the medics. They take off for the
hospital. Another unit is they're assisting me with the mother. We have not told
her much yet about the baby. Only that we are taking both of them to the hospital. We get the mother in the back of the other unit. And we head to the hospital.
I am driving my unit to the hospital.

I get to the hospital. I am a little upset. We find out that the baby died. Keith
gets back in the truck. We head back to the station with out giving a signal. At
the station I walk in. I am very upset. Keith is still in the bus. Lieutenant Missel is
on the desk.

"Is it the last job you did"? He ask

"Yes sir"

I start to cry. It is the hardest thing to deal with. Keith is outside in the truck. He is crying about the call to. Lieutenant Missel puts us out of service and calls for the counciling unit to respond to the station. We will be off service for the rest of the shift. The counciling unit arrives and starts talking to us. It helps but you still feel upset about the call. It makes you wonder about the job.

ITS SPRINGTIME

Well spring has finally arrived. It is starting to get warm out. I have survived the winter and the blizzard. I decide to ride my motorcycle to work today. It is so nice out that I don't even want to go to work. But I have to. It will take me about fifteen minutes to get there. I am working with Oscar Stack today. Oscar is a lot of fun to work with. He is studying to become a nurse. Oscar lives in queens and knows the area pretty well. He does not like to use the map and generally knows where he is going. We are working up in the mainland today.

"Four-Zero-Boy for the hypertension at 23543 Seven Seven Street cross street Two Three Avenue. You have a seventy-five year old female with hypertension" the dispatcher tells us.

"Ten-four sixty-three" Oscar responds over the radio.

We take off for the call. I have no idea where we are going other then it is in the Forest Hill section of Queens. We get there in about ten minutes. There is an elderly lady waiting for us in the living room.

"I called my blood pressure is high. I really do not want to go to the hospital. If I have to go can you take me to Parkway Hospital please?" she states.

"Sure we can" Oscar replies.

He whisper to me "Hey Cali where is Parkway Hospital"?

"I think it is near the parkway off Queens Boulevard" I rely.

"Ok got it"

"I want to walk to the ambulance" she states.

"Ok but I need you to sign the release on the back of this report"

She does and we head back out to the ambulance. Oscar looks up the hospital number and types the information into the computer. We take off for the hospital. We have been enroute for about fifteen minutes. When the patient ask me.

"Are you sure he knows how to get to the hospital. You just passed my house".

"He knows how to get there. We are driving you around to get your blood pressure down. So you will not have to stay there" I reply.

"That's nice of you thank you because I do not want to stay there" she replies.

We drive for about another ten minutes. All the sudden Oscar calls out.

"I found it; it is just around the corner".

We take her into the emergency room. It is the first time we have been here. It is a nice hospital. Everybody is friendly. The nurse comes out sign for the patient. She takes her over to the triage area.

We go back outside and get in the bus.

"That hospital was a pain in the ass to find" Oscar states.

"Yea it took you a while. I told her we were driving her around to get her blood pressure down" I reply.

"That's a good one"

We go available and start heading back to our area. Oscar is a pro with the computer and knows how to get us to where we need to go. He believes in taking care of all personal business on duty. And so do I. From there we have to go to Quartermaster to pick up uniform jackets that were order for us.

Since the fire department merger, we now get all our uniforms issued to us. We don't have to by them. That saves us money. But you have to go to the Quartermaster to pick them up. Oscar punches in different locations into the computer. We are able to get to Quartermaster pick up are jackets without a problem. This is great one less thing to do on my day off. This takes us about an hour. The rest of the shift is nothing happens and we head back to the station.

"Hey Rob what's up"? I ask as I walk into the station.

"Not much how was your days off" he replies.

As I walk into the station. I have been off for the last five days. I tend to do mutual where you work two double shifts and single shift. Then you are off five days at a time.

It felt good to get away for a while. Tour two is on a late job and will not be back for at least an hour. They are at Jamaica Hospital up on the mainland. And will hit rush hour traffic all the way back to the station. I go in the lounge and kick back. They finally get back. They are going off. So we will restock the unit when we check it out. Rob tells the dispatcher we will be late logging on. It takes us about thirty minutes to get the unit back in service.

"Four-Zero-Boy and Four-Three-Xray for the cardiac arrest. You have an arrest at 156 Avenue and Crossbay in the motel" the dispatcher tells us.

"Four-Zero-Boy ten four sixty three"

We are already on Crossbay Boulevard so it is a straight shot for us. We should be there in three minutes. We pull up in front of the motel. We grab our equipment and the stretcher and head into the building.

"It is room 1515" the clerk yells to us.

We take the elevator to the fifteenth floor. We get out and there is the patient lying on the floor. I check for airway, breathing, and a pulse. They are all absent.

"We have a confirmed arrest," I yell to Rob

Rob tells the dispatcher and starts setting up the defilbator. I rip his shirt and expose his chest. Rob puts the pads on his chest and gets ready to shock the patient.

"Stand clear to shock all clear" Rob yells.

He presses the button. The body jumps a little. I check he has a very weak pulse. I measure a put an airway. Then we get ready to start bagging him. We can hear the medics coming down the hallway.

"What's going on" they ask.

"We shocked him once and we got a pulse back" I rely.

"Ok let's get some medication in him. Does anybody have any information on him"? They ask.

"Just his name and address" I reply.

"Ok Cali go see what you can find" they tell me.

I start looking through the room for any information. All the time I have a police officer with me. There is no way I am going to get accused of taking anything. After a couple minutes I come out and tell them I found nothing.

"Ok we will take him to hospital thirty-four" they say.

We start preparing him for transportation to the hospital. I am moving furniture around to get him out. We load the patient on to the stretcher. He is not heavy so he is not hard to move. We are back down and in the back of the ambulance in about ten minutes. It will be about a fifteen-minute ride to the hospital. Rob gets in the driver seat. I jump in the back with the medic. The other unit will notify the hospital. By this time he is starting to breathe on his own. This will be my first prehospital save. We start heading to the hospital. It is a straight shot for us. Crossbay to the Belt Parkway to the Van Wyck Expressway to Jamaica Avenue. We get there in about fifteen minutes. The patient is doing a little better now.

Rob backs the ambulance into the emergency room entrance. We unload the stretcher. The cardiac team is they're waiting for us. The patient is still unconscious. But he is still alive. The medics are giving their report to the team. We move the patient on to the hospital stretcher. I start filling out the rest of my paperwork. Rob is busy changing the oxygen tank and cleaning up the back of the bus. It feels really good getting my first prehospital save. I finish my paperwork get it signed and head back out to the bus. I will get my certificate at the station in couple of weeks.

As I walk into the station.

Lieutenant Missel calls out "Hey Cali I have your Prehospital Save Certificate and bar for you".

"Thanks sir" I reply.

He gives me an envelope with the certificate and a red and yellow bar. These are the colors for the prehospital save. It has been a month since the arrest. The last I heard the man was doing fine. But I really do not check up on patients.

It is getting warmer outside. You can feel the warm breeze off the ocean as you go to work everyday. It is nice working tour three. You can hang out late get up late still go to the beach and be at work on time. People are starting to come to the beach on weekends. So they have moved are unit back down to Rockaway for the summer. We will be down here all summer. I will miss the rides up to the mainland. But oh well such is life in the big city.

It is a warm Saturday. I am working a double so I can have an extra day off during the week. It is around twelve noon when I look up. You can smell smoke in the air. I look to the west you can see smoke in the area that has small houses.

"Oh shit Rob looks like there is a fire over around Beach Seventy-eight Street, lets go check it out"

We start heading in that direction. We look for a second time and see a large cloud of smoke to the east of us towards Long Island. It looks close to Saint Johns Hospital. All the sudden the radio comes to life. The dispatcher tells all Rockaway units to go to Citywide.

We switch are radio to Citywide. There is a lot of talk on the radio. You can hear chiefs responding down here. They are talking about two major fires and a major accident in the area.

"Four-Zero-Boy to Citywide"

"Four-Zero-Boy respond to Beach One Three Street and Congo for the structural fire" the dispatcher tells us.

"Four-Zero-Boy Citywide ten-four sixty-three"

We turn on our lights and sirens and starting heading to the job. We are heading down Beach Channel Drive toward the job. You van hear a lot of sirens. We are seeing companies that you do not see in Rockaway. It takes us about three minutes to get to the fire.

"Four-Zero-Boy to Citywide"

"Citywide go ahead Four-Zero-Boy"

"Four-Zero-Boy to Citywide we have an abandon building three stories high one hundred fifty feet by two hundred feet fully involved in fire. Fire operating on scene, no patients at this time end of report".

"Ten four Four-Zero-Boy"

We will be here for a while. It is a hot and humid day so there will be some heat exhaustion cases. You can hear the other units giving reports on the radio.

We set an area for triage and treatment of injured personal. You can hear more sirens as more units respond into the Rock. See Rockaway is a small island connected to the mainland by two bridges. Or you have drive through Nassau County to get here. We only have six engine companies, three ladder companies and four ambulances assigned down here, and according to the radio two major fires and a major accident working on this small island. This will definitely put Rockaway on the map today.

Well it is getting close to the end of the first shift. I still have another eight hours to go. They are starting to wrap up from the fire. There have been no injuries to report. So all we had to do was standby. We will be heading back to the station soon. It definitely was an interesting shift. My second shift nothing major happen. So you could say it was an easy double. Personally I am glad it is over. We go back to the station. I take my uniform off jump on my Ninga and head home for four days off.

It is close to when school closes for the summer. There are children all over the place. All the sudden the radio comes to life.

"Four-Zero-Boy, Four-One-Boy, Four-One-Xray, Four-One Patrol respond to the school bus accident. Report of a school bus into a pole at Beach Two Two Nine Street and Beach Channel Drive. All units responding switch to Citywide" the dispatcher tells us.

"Four-Zero-Boy Citywide sixty-three"

"Ten-four"

We start heading west on Beach channel drive. It is at the far end of the island. I am thinking about all the children that could be injured. I hope it is nothing major. We get there in about six minutes. Patrol Four-One is already on the scene, and has assumed command. We hear him over the radio telling Citywide that it is a minor accident. That the two volunteer ambulances in the community are treating the patients. And that all units can go back in service.

I look to my side and there is Engine 309 in the sand. The engine is stuck. There is sand up to the frame. I feel sorry them they will have to get a tow truck to get them out. Our shift is almost over. By the time we get back to the station it will be time to go home.

HAZ-TEC ACADEMY

"Hey Cali you got your orders for Haz-Tec training" Captain Roberts tells me as I enter the station.

"Ok sir when do I report"

"In two weeks to Fort Totten"

"Got it sir"

Cool I go after I get back from vacation. I go in and clean out my locker. And load everything in the back of my truck since I will not becoming back here. I am wondering where I will be assigned. I hope that I will have good partners. That is the most important part of this job.

It is my first day at Haz-Tec training. I leave my apartment early and head to the academy. It is different working during the day. I am use to working the graveyard shift, and sleeping in the mourning. I stop by the bagel store and get breakfast. Then it is off to the forty-five minutes drive to the academy. All the time I am thinking about what I will be doing there for the next three weeks. I arrive a little early and park my truck, kick back and relax. There are other vehicles pulling in know. Well it is time to go into the academy and find my classroom. I will go in and find a seat in the back of the class. I do not like working days. I like my days free.

In comes Chief McBlade he is in charge of the Special Operations Command for the fire department.

"Good mourning everybody, welcome to the Special Operations Command Haz-Mat Unit. You will be trained to the specialist level in hazardous materials" he tells us.

He goes on to explain about the job. What all of our training will consist of. The mission of both special operations and the hazardous materials unit. He then introduces us to the personal that will be training us. I am looking at the schedule that they passed out to us. They tell us we must pass mask confidence to stay in the class.

I am in the back row half-asleep by now. I am sitting next to Rene Barns and Zelda Robert on one side and Mike Johnson on the other side. The next thing I know Zelda taps me on the shoulder and tells me.

"Wake up your falling asleep" she whispers.

It is time for a fifteen-minute break. Great I can go outside and get some fresh air and wake up. The next thing I know it is time to head back into the classroom.

Captain Flash comes in the room.

"Good mourning we are going to cover incident command, start, and hazardous materials incident management systems. This will take about three hours" he tells us.

I get out my notebook and start taking notes. He is putting a lot of important information. And we will be tested on it later on. It is a long three hours. I can't wait for the next break.

It is time for our next class. It is called Introduction to Chemistry. And will include the following subtitles Periodic chart, Ionic and Covalent Bonding, Chemical Families, and Chemical and Physical Properties. This class is three days long. It will start when we get back from lunch. I am starting to think, what did I get back myself into. This is only one day and I still have three weeks left. The next thing I know it is time for lunch. I head down to the local Seven-Eleven and by a Diet Coke to wake me up. I know it will be a long afternoon. We come back from lunch and enter the classroom. There are charts and graphs all over the place. I feel like I am back in chemistry in high school or college. I liked chemistry when I was in school. It is a long afternoon. Well it is finally three o'clock in the afternoon and time to go home. Day one is over and only fourteen days left.

I arrive a little early for my fourth day of class. The first thing we have as soon as class starts is a test. We are given one hour for the one hundred-question test. It covers everything from the first day. It takes me about forty-five minutes to complete the test. Our results will be posted after lunch. Day four will consist of Awareness and Safety in the mourning and after lunch it will be Operations. Captain Flash is teaching the class. I am sitting in my seat in the back of the class. I will try and stay awake. It will be hard to do. I am still not used to working during the day. I make it through the day. Tomorrow will be fun we will be working with self contained breathing apparatus for the next couple of days.

Today we head over to the smokehouse. It is a metal building that is all black. Firefighter Rush is our instructor. He explains that we have to pass the written and practical test to continue training. The first four hours he will explain how the pack works and the different parts. Then we will be given a written test before lunch. When we get back from lunch, we will be wearing the air packs and working with them. It will be a lot of fun. After lunch I check the list. I have passed the written test.

We are now starting to wear and work with the air packs. We have to learn how to do a side profile, low profile, and take the pack off and put it on blind folded. We will be practicing this for the next four hours. We are still not allowed in the smokehouse yet. It is about two in the afternoon.

Firefighter Rush tells us "Line up it is time to start testing".

We get in a line and start performing the different task with the air pack. I get through the practical test without a problem.

"Ok people tomorrow we start going into the smokehouse with your face piece covered. You will not be able to see anything. Wear old clothes because you will get dirty and sweat. See all of you in the mourning. Class dismissed" firefighter Rush tells us.

It is the second day at the mask training area. Today we will be going inside the metal black buildings and crawling around. This simulates that you are in a building full of smoke. In the mourning we will go into the building and performing the different task we have learned. Then in the afternoon we will go in and try and find a baby mannequin. It will not be easy to do. But we have to pass this to continue in the class. It is coming up to my turn.

I put on my air pack.

"Ok go on air and find the baby" firefighter Rush tell us.

I go on air. You can feel the air coming into mask. It pressurizes the mask. You can feel the air against your face. This is to prevent any gasses from outside the mask getting into the mask. I am going in with Mike Johnson he is my partner.

"Hey are you ready"? Mike asks.

"Yea lets go" I reply.

We enter the building duck walking. This is where you walk with you knees bent. It very uncomfortable and hard to do. The face pieces we are wearing are painted black. I can't even see my hand in front of my face. It is really hot and I am sweating like a pig. Mike is right behind me. He is holding the back of my tank with one hand. I now we are in a hallway. I feel a doorway and go to the right. I keep one hand on the wall at all times. All the time I am sweeping the area with my left hand and foot. I feel a couch; I sweep across the top and the bottom. Still I do not feel anything out of the ordinary. We are working are way around the room always keeping are right side against the wall. This is so we do not get lost in the room. It feels a lot different not being able to see anything. After a couple of minutes we finishing searching the living room and are moving back into the hallway. I feel another opening.

I feel through the door, it feels like a bathroom. I can feel the toilet. I sweep behind the toilet. All the sudden I feel something. It feels like a pair of legs.

"Hey Mike I got a body" I yell.

I can feel a face. I pull the body from behind the toilet. We start working are way back out of the building. We finally get to where you can feel a breeze. We are now outside the building.

"Ok you men can go off air" the instructor tells us.

We take off our face piece. And turn off the air bottles.

"It took you guys twenty minutes to find the baby very good" he tells us.

It was the longest twenty minutes for me in a long time. It was a lot of fun. We will be doing this type of drill for the next two days.

It is a lot of fun. After you do your drill you get to kick back and relax before you go again. Each crew does the drill at least eight times a day. The mannequin is always in a different location and the change the layout around each time. We are starting to get very proficient with our air packs. We have to pass this class to move to the next unit of our training. Inside the building they have areas where you have to take the air pack off and slide it through an opening and then put it back on. In one area it feels like the floor is missing and you have to straddle the beams to make it through. There are areas where you can hardly fit through. In all it is very educational and fun. When we get done for the day we are tired and dirty. All you want to do is take a shower, go home and relax.

Well our three days of working with the air packs is over. Everybody has passed. The next unit of our training is wearing and working in the suits. We will start doing that tomorrow. It should be interesting and fun. I arrive at that the academy early it is cool outside. So the suit will not be to hot I hope. In comes Lieutenant Fisk.

"Good mourning I am Lieutenant Fisk. I will be teaching the following subjects this mourning. They are Introduction to Chemical Protective Clothing, use limitations, descriptions of level of clothing, equipment needs by level, and differences in levels. After we get done with the lecture we will break for lunch. You will have to breaks during this lecture. After lunch you will be working with the suits. Are there any questions? Also how did everybody like the smokehouse?" he states to us.

He starts his lecture. I am sitting in the back row against the wall. The next thing I now Zelda is hitting me.

"Wake up" she whispers me.

Both Rene and I are asleep. I have gotten to the point I can sleep anywhere. I still have not gotten use to working during the day. It is rough getting up and trying to stay awake during class. I hope that when I get done training I will be back on Tour One. Finally it is lunchtime. I head down to Seven-Eleven to get something to wake me up. I also pick up some breath mints.

We get back from lunch. There are Level A chemical suits and air packs lined on the floor. These types of suits are heavy and have a fireproof outer lining. This is the type of suit we will be working with.

"Ok everybody pair up" the lieutenant tells us.

It will be Mike Johnson and myself.

"Hey Cali you can go first" Mike states.

"Ok"

"Let me help you with the air pack"

"Got it up on my shoulders, let me tighten up the straps"

"Ok"

"Let start putting on the suit, I will hold it up and you can step in to it"

"Ok Mike"

We start putting on the suit. It is very heavy and stiff. This should be a lot of fun to work in.

"Ok everybody listen up. We are going to go on air. Then we are going to go through an obstacle course in the suit. This to get you use to the suit" the lieutenant tells us.

I start moving in the suit. It feels heavy and is hard to move in. I can hear and feel the air coming into mask. We take off in a line. First we have to climb to the second floor on an escape ladder. I climb up the ladder and on to a landing. Then we have to go through a window. After that we walk back down the stairs and head toward the drill field. There are seven different tasks we have to perform in the suit.

As we head toward the field you can feel the suit getting hot inside. This is because when you are in the suit. You are sealed off from the outside environment. So when you exhale the warm air stays inside with you. I get over to the field. I am sweating inside the suit. I have to duck walk for about one hundred feet. Then I have to seal a barrel with a plug kit. Then I have to place the drum upright. From there I have to move a mannequin on to a sked. This is a sled that we use to move an unconscious or injured person from a contaminated area. After placing the mannequin on the sked I have to drag it one hundred feet to the finish line. It takes about twenty minutes to go through the course. I finally get done. It is real hot inside the suit now. Mike is there to help me out of the suit.

"Hey Cali how was it"?

"Not to bad just you sweat like a pig inside the suit. Ok Mike it is you turn now. I will help you with the air pack and into the suit"

"Ok let go for it" Mike replies.

Mike starts putting on the air pack and suit. It is now time for him to go through the course. We will each go through the course at least four times today. All this is to get you use to wearing and working in the suits. You are not allowed to kneel in the suits. This is because you could rip the suit. And that would cause major problems. Mike finally gets done with the course.

"Are you ready to come out of the suit"? I ask.

"Yea"

I start getting him out of the suit.

"Man the cool air feels good" he replies.

He is dripping wet with sweat. We go over and get a cup of cold water. It is almost time to hit the showers and clean up for the day. Since it is Friday I will be off for the weekend. We are about half way through the training. It will feel good to get back to the field.

Well it is Monday mourning and I am back at the academy. We enter the classroom and I take my seat in the back row. Hopefully I will be able to do a better job at staying awake now. In comes Lieutenant Flask.

"Good mourning everybody, this mourning we are going to cover the following subjects Decontamination principals, types, responder, victims and equipment. We will have to breaks then lunch. After lunch we will be in the suits. Are there any questions? Ok lets get started".

He starts his lecture. I am taking notes and I brought my breath mints to keep me awake. They seam to be working. He is giving us a lot of information on decontamination. It is very interesting. I am staying awake during the whole class. That is a first. I guess the breath mints are working. The next thing I know it is time for lunch. I head down to the store to buy some Gaterade to drink. It is hot and humid out. So it will be and sweaty in the suits today. But at least we will be able to cool off with a hose line. Today we are decontaminating patients with water. We each perform the deacon drill four times. Then it is time to hit the showers and go home. The showers always feel good.

"Good mourning class, today we are going to cover tools, equipment, and rad50 meters. Then lunch and after lunch we will be in level B suits today" firefighter Rush tell us.

He starts talking about the different tools we will be using. It is already the second break. After the break we will be going over radiation detectors. The Rad50 detector we clip to our suits. It will tell us the amount of radiation the suits are being exposed to. The mourning class goes by pretty fast. It was pretty interesting and fun. Firefighter Rush gave us a lot of information. The next thing I now it is lunchtime, and after lunch we will spend the rest day in the suits.

This afternoon should not be too bad. We are using level B protective suits. They are used for splash protection. You are still sealed from the outside environment. But they are not heavy and bulky like level suits. I can put my suit without help. All I need Mike to do is seal the back of the suit. Mike is there if I need him. We go out and perform a small deacon drill. They are starting to use scenarios for the drills. It is starting to look like a hazardous materials incident. The drills are becoming more fun. We only have three more days of class left. Then a final written test and last week is all drills.

As I enter the academy. They have written on the board what are lecture will be for the mourning class. Today is medical monitoring and toxicology. The instructor is Captain Flash. I go sit down in the back row. I am getting use to staying awake in class. If I do fall asleep there is always Zelda there to wake me up. In comes Captain Flash.

"Good mourning everybody, today we will be talking about medical monitoring and toxicology. Are they any question? Ok lets get started"

He starts his lecture. It has been a long four hours. We have two breaks. I try and wake myself but it is not happening. Zelda keeps hitting my shoulder and waking me up. Finally it is lunchtime. I go get my Geterade for lunch. This is because it is hot out, and you sweat real bad in the suits. We will be in suits all afternoon.

"Ok everybody fall outside" he tells us.

There is a large deacon tractor-trailer outside.

"Today we will be working with the deacon trailer. This is Deacon One it is station in Lower Manhattan with Fifteen Truck" he tells us.

Captain Flash starts to explain the truck to us. He starts going in detail on how to set it up. What filters are needed and where they are placed. How to monitor the water run off from the truck. The class is very interesting. It takes the rest of the afternoon. The next thing I now it is time to go home. Cool no suit time today. I jump in my truck by a soda and head to my house.

Today in class we are doing bag-valve mask, cervical spine immobilization and mark one administration. Then we will be in suits for the rest of the day. The class will only be two hours long. There is a nice breeze blowing off the water. So it will be a little cooler today. Lieutenant Flask is teaching the class. He enters the room and starts giving his lecture. After the first break we head out to the drill area. I am working with Mike my partner.

"Hey Mike you can go first this time"

"Thanks Cali I will remember this" he replies.

"Ready for the air pack"?

"Yea got it; let me get into the suit"

He starts putting the suit. I assist him and seal the back.

"Ok everybody go on air" the lieutenant tells us.

We head out to the drill area. There are mannequins on the ground. They each weigh about one hundred and eighty pounds. The object of the drill is to place the mannequin on a backboard and take it to the deacon area. There we place the mannequin and backboard in a tub of water and wash it off. Each drill takes about twenty minutes to do. Mikes bell on his air pack starts ringing. This tells him he only has five minutes of air left. He has to leave the area. He and his partner head out to the cool zone. First he sprayed off with water. This is to remove any contamination on him. Then he goes over to the staging area.

"Hear have a seat. Let's start getting you out of the suit" I tell him.

He sits down. I start helping him get the suit off. He is wet with sweat. He then takes the mask off.

"Man that air feels good. It's your turn now have fun. It's a ball buster" Mike states.

I start getting ready. First I put the air pack on. Then I step into the suit. It is hot bulking and full of sweat.

"Ok everybody go on air" the lieutenant tells us.

We head over to the drill area. The suit is stiff to walk in. there are mannequins all over the area. We have to do the same thing as the group before us. The object is to roll them on to a backboard and then take them to the deacon area.

There we have to lift them and put them in a deacon tub. I stoop down with another student to get ready and perform the skill.

"Ok are you ready, I got the head," I yell.

"Yea lets go" he replies.

We slide the board up against the mannequin. I grab the head and my partner grabs the thigh area.

"Ok on the count of three we roll the mannequin on to the board, one, two three" I yell.

We roll the mannequin on to the board. It is not an easy thing to do. Then we secure the mannequin to the board with the straps. We are in a squatting position now.

"Ok on three we stand up and head to the deacon area" I yell.

"Got it," he yells at me.

"Ok one, two, three up" I yell.

We stand up and start heading toward the deacon area. It is not easy to do. I can feel the sweat dripping off me. I am drained of energy. It takes all my energy to get through the objective. I am soaken wet inside the suit. We finally make it to the deacon area.

There we place the board and the mannequin in the tube. And we start washing it down with water and soap. After a couple of minutes of washing, we pick up the mannequin and board and move it to a clean area. This where the patient is turned over to an ambulance crew. Then I head to the deacon trailer for a shower. The water feels good flowing over the suit. It takes about twenty minutes to perform the drill. I am dripping wet with sweat as Mike show up to help me out of the suit. Once out of the suit the cool breeze feels good. We will perform the drill again after lunch.

After lunch we get ready to do more drills. We also have to use the Mark Two kits now. These kits contain medication to use in different types of chemical attacks. We each get to drill three more times. The drills are all the same in the mourning. They might change the scenario a little. We will be performing drills for the next four days.

Captain Flash tells us "You can expect six drills a day. Three before lunch and three after lunch".

We are in our last couple of days at the academy. It has been an interesting three weeks. I have had a good time and learned a lot. We have a final written test this mourning. Then we get a break. When we come back we will go over the test. Then after lunch we will have a final drill. The test was a hundred question multiple choice. I did not think it was hard. After the break we come in. the grades are posted by social security number. I see that I scored a ninety-eight on the test. So I passed. After lunch we do our final drill in the suits. It was not bad. And of course it was hot and sweaty. Then we take our showers. All that is left is a lecture from Doctor Gush. Then after that a tabletop exercise. It has not been a bad three weeks. I learned a lot.

I have been assigned to the Four Nine Battalion in Queens. It is a new station opening up in Astoria section of Queens. It should be fun working at a new station. I will help get to design the station patch and logo.

FIRST HAZ-MAT JOB

I leave my house early to head to work. I do not now this area of Queens. While I am driving to he station. I am thinking about what will the captain be like. I do not now this captain. What are the people like that are assigned the station. Will I be able to do mutuals? This is all going through my mind as I drive to the station. It takes me about an hour to get to work. The station is a small building behind the hospital. So it is not easy find and parking is a problem to. I finally find the station and I find a parking place without much trouble. I head down the stairs to the station.

"Hi my name is James Thompson I am assigned the Haz-Tec unit here"

"No problem come on in make yourself at home. My name is John I am assigned Four-Nine-Adam. The captain here is Captain Cake she is pretty easy going and fun to work under. I am not sure who the lieutenants are. Go ahead find a locker and put your information on it" John tells me.

I head into the locker room. There are nice new lockers in the room. Not what I am used to. They say the captain is pretty good. She approves mutuals as long as you get your forty hours in a week. This is great I have already found a mutual partner. I think I am really going to like this station.

I am assigned to Four-Nine-Henry Tour One. I will be working eleven at night to seven in the mourning. That works our great for me.

"Hey Cali can you work overtime Tour Two today"? The lieutenant asks.

"Yes sir no problem" I reply.

"You are working with Ken Bash on the Haz-Tec unit" he replies.

Ken was in my Haz-Tec class. I worked with him in Far Rockaway Queens. Mourning comes it was a quite night.

I leave my gear on the truck.

"Hey Cali you can drive today" Ken tells me

"Ok go ahead and log us on" I reply.

"Did you guys do any jobs last night"? Ken asks

"No it was a quite night we did not turn a wheel" I reply.

Ken does a real fast check of all the equipment. Goes in and gets the lieutenants signature. And we are off to McDonalds for breakfast.

"Four-Nine-Henry switch to Citywide for the hazardous materials assignment" the radio calls out.

"Four-Nine-Henry ten four, Four-Nine-Henry to Citywide for the assignment"

"Four-Nine-Henry respond to Purdy Street off Treatmont for the hazardous materials incident" Citywide tells us.

"Ten four sixty three"

"Ken do you know anything about the Bronx"? I ask

"Nope only that the Whitestone, Tribourgh, and Trogs Neck Bridge go there" he replies.

This should be interesting I do not now anything about the Bronx other then the same information. Ken gets out the map and starts looking up the location.

"Ok take the Tribourgh Bridge into the Bronx. It looks like it will put us close to the call" Ken tells me.

I am heading over the bridge towards the Bronx.

"Where do I get off at"?

"I do not know. I cannot find the street she gave us" Ken replies.

"Which one the street the job is on? Oh shit we are entering the Bronx. Do you see where we are on the map"?

"Yea but I cannot find the job location" Ken replies.

"Keep looking"

"I am"

We are getting off the bridge and heading north on the Brunker Expressway now.

"It looks like you can take the Brunker up and get off on Treatmont Street" Ken replies.

"Ok where do I go from there"?

"Hold on let me see if I can find Purdy Street. I do not see it. Take Treatmont we can follow it to Purdy" ken replies.

"Ok sounds good to me".

It now has been ten minutes into the response. All we know is we are in the Bronx and on Treatmont Avenue. The Bronx is very confusing. The map will show streets that are through streets. You go down them for a couple of blocks. Then all the sudden there is an apartment building blocking the street. After about twenty minutes we are heading down Treatmont to correct direction to Purdy. It is a small street and hard to find on the map. We are starting to see a lot of fire and police vehicles.

"Hey we found it. Hit the eighty-eight button and put us on the scene".

"Yea"

The squad is there. They tell us that it was a boiler explosion and the area is contaminated with asbestos. They show us where to park over in the support area. And that we are to go ahead and suit up. But we are not on go on air yet. We start getting all equipment out. First we put on the jump suits and air packs. Then we pull out the bag with the level B splash suits. There is a lot of old buildings and steam pipes in the city that has asbestos on them. Asbestos is a carcinogen that you can inhale that causes cancer of the lungs. It is very nasty stuff.

We get our suits on and head over the deacon trailer. We will be in the deacon trailer deaconing the firefighters. We will work in the suits for about twenty minutes. Then another crew will come in and relieve us. This job will take the rest of day. We now have been operating at the job for about an hour. Thank goodness it is not hot and humid today. It is a nice cool day with a breeze. It is now around two in the afternoon. We have been out the job for about five hours.

"Hey you guys are a fifteen hundred unit correct" Lieutenant Flask asks us.

"Yes sir" I reply.

"Ok go ahead and start heading back to Queens, I am releasing you. I will tell Citywide". Lieutenant Flask tells us.

I am all hot and sweaty now. I can not wait to get back to the station and take a shower. We start heading back to the station. The rush hour is starting so traffic is backing up. So it will take us at least an hour to get to the station.

It takes us an hour and a half to get to the station. The other crew is they're waiting for us. They will go ahead and replace all the equipment we used. It feels good to take a shower and get ready to go home. It will take me about an hour and half to get to my house in Long Beach. I am off for the next five days so I will kick back and relax.

"Four-Nine-Henry respond to Roosevelt Island for carbon monoxide in the subway tunnel" the dispatcher tells us.

"Ten four responding" I reply.

This call is easy to get to. All we have to do is head south on Twenty-First Street and turn right on Thirty-seven Avenue and we are there. We get there in a couple of minutes.

The Battalion Chief tells us "We need you to stand by, there should be no patients. We have turned on the fans to ventilate the tunnel. So just stand by till the gas dissipates"

"Yes sir"

Tim and I just kick back and relax. This is one of those easy jobs where you just stand by. You do not need to suit up. All you have to do is wait for the all clear. We are at the job for about forty-five minutes. We get cleared and start heading back to the station. We will be back in time for lunch.

It is starting to get cool out. You can feel the fall breeze. I am working a double tonight. The afternoon shift was pretty quite. We had a couple of jobs. But the re was nothing exciting. The one thing I despise about this station is. You get assigned all the jobs on Rikers Island. This is where New York City houses all its prisoners. It is a large prison complex on an island. You can only enter of a bridge that is about a mile long. It is about one in the mourning. There is a movie on television. I am not paying any attention to it. All the sudden the radio calls out.

"Four-Nine-Adam, Four-Nine-Charlie, and Four-Nine-Henry respond to Rikers Island for the bus crash. We have a report of fifteen correction officers injured. Also conditions Four-Six is responding"

Tim and I start heading toward Rikers Island. We will be there in about five minutes. We get to the checkpoint and stop. The guards give us clearance to the bridge. At the end of the bridge we meet a patrol unit that takes us to the accident scene. We arrive at the accident scene in about five minutes. All the patients are in a building. They all have minor injuries and are walking wounded. Conditions Four-Six have set up a transport area. We are to take four walking wounded to Elmhurst Hospital. This is an easy job. We start filling out all the paperwork. I then get up front and we take an easy ride to the hospital. It takes us about fifteen minutes to get to the hospital.

We get to the hospital drop off the patients. The triage nurse signs for them. It is a full moon out and the night is just starting. The bars will be closing soon and it could be a busy night. But it is a quite night. Rikers is the only job we have all night. I head home in the morning for eight hours. Then it will be back for another double shift.

I come in to the station. They have put a helm at the entrance to the station in the lobby.

"We came up with the name The Submarine Station, since we are in the basement of the building. We thought the name would fit us well. The station patch is going to look like a submarine." Bob tells me.

"Ok it should be interesting" I reply.

One good thing about the station is. People can not find it to bother you. I grab my gear and head out to my unit. I am the technician today. So I get the joy of checking all the equipment in the back and filling out the checklist. It will take me about thirty minutes to do. Then we will head out for breakfast.

"Hey Cali are you about ready to hit the streets for breakfast"?

"Four-Nine-Henry switch to Citywide for the hazardous materials assignment"

"Four-Nine-Henry to Citywide"

"Four-Nine-Henry respond to Public School Seven-Zero-Two for seventy-five sick children" the dispatcher tells us.

"Four-Nine-Henry ten four responding" I reply.

"Yea let me get the checklist signed"

"Ok I will be waiting for you in the unit" Tim replies.

It is on the other side of Queens near JFK Airport. It will take us at least thirty minutes to get there. We start heading towards the school. We are heading down the Grand Central parkway. Our lights and sirens are on. People are moving to the side for us. The parkway is not crowed so we are making good time. We are coming up to the merge with the Van Wyck Expressway. Traffic is a little backed up now. We get on the Van Wyck Expressway.

We head out of the station for McDonalds. It is about four blocks from the station. As we are heading down the street the radio calls us.

"Four-Nine-Henry switch to Citywide for the hazardous materials assignment"

"Four-Nine-Henry to Citywide"

"Four-Nine-Henry respond to Public School Seven Two for seventy-five sick children" the dispatcher tells us.

"Four-Nine-Henry ten four responding"

It is on the other side of Queens. It will take us thirty minutes to get there. We start heading toward the Grand central Parkway. The parkway is not crowed so we are making good time. We are heading toward the merge with the Van Wyck expressway. Traffic is starting to back up a little. We get on the Van Wyck and head toward the airport. Traffic is not that bad. We get off on Foch street exit. The school is about eight blocks away now. We get to the scene in about twenty minutes.

Conditions Five-Four is on the scene with about six ambulances.

"I need you guys to set up a transport sector and do tracking on all the patients. We have a carbon monoxide leak from a boiler" he tells us.

"No problem" I reply.

We pull out all the equipment we need. We will take down the entire patients name and what hospital they are going to. We will also keep track the ambulances and how many patients go to each hospital. The medical officer on the scene states there are to be four patients to each ambulance. The first ambulance pulls up we copy down all the information. The ambulance takes off for the hospital.

I keep doing this to all the patients are transported to the hospital. We end up using a total of twenty ambulances. My hand is getting tired of writing. Tim is talking on the radio to Citywide getting up dates from the hospital. We are just about finished. The condition boss finally releases us. We finish up all our paperwork and start heading back to the station for lunch. We were not able to grab breakfast. That is why I always grab something on the way to work.

It is December now and it is cold in Queens. I am working the night shift overtime with Linda Smith. She is a lot of fun to work with. We are just hanging out waiting for a job. We hear Four-Five-Boy get an abdominal pain at Twenty-First Street and Thirty-Fifth Avenue. We are close to the job but it is not for us.

"Hey Cali lets take the job" Linda states.

"No problem I do not care" I reply.

The dispatcher tells the other unit to disregard the job and gives it to us. She sends us over all the information. It tells us we have a twenty-one year old female with abdominal pain and is vomiting. We are about five blocks away and head over to the job. It takes us about two minutes to get there. I grab my equipment and Linda grabs the chair and we head in to the apartment building. We find the apartment and ring the bell. A lady answers the door.

"It's my daughter she is on the couch" she tells us.

Since it is a female Linda starts asking all the questions. She hands me the insurance card. Her name is Irene and birthday is five days before mine.

"We both have December birthdays" I state.

"Yes I guess we do" she replies.

"Do you want to sit in the chair or walk to the ambulance"? Linda asks.

"I will walk to the ambulance" she replies.

I am making small talk with her as we head to the hospital. Her mother is in the ambulance with her. She is giving me the meanest looks possible. We take her up the street to the hospital. It is only a five-minute ride. So I really do not get to say much to her. I escort her to the triage desk and start giving the nurse all the information. Her mother is still giving me dirty looks. They take her back into the treatment area. Linda and I head back to the station. A little while later we head back to the hospital emergency room.

"Hey I see you are still here" I say.

"Yes they think it is my appendix, I might be here for my birthday" she replies.

We start talking more. I tell her about my December birthday we have at my house. I have five friends that have December birthdays. So we have one big party for them all. I ask her if she wants to come. We talk more she finally gives me her number. She tells me what she likes and does not like. If she is still in the hospital I am going to give her a firefighter teddy bear. She tells me about her teddy bear collection.

It is now about five in the morning. I will be getting off work at seven. Only two more hours to go. Around six we get dispatched for a job. We get there and it turns out to be a false alarm. On the way back to the station we stop by the hospital. I go to see if Irene is still in the emergency room. I find out that she was discharged and went home.

I wake up about one in the afternoon. It is a cold winter day out. I decide to give Irene a call. I find her number and give her a call. She tells me about her experience in the emergency room last night. We talk for about an hour on the phone and decide to see each other again. I go and pick her up at her house. We take off for a little while. We decide to stop and get something to drink. Her birthday is in three days.

It is Irene'S birthday today. I go to the store and buy her a nice card. Then I go to a bear store and buy her a firefighter teddy bear. I ask the lady to wrap it in birthday paper so I can take it to her. I have to work tonight so we cannot hangout on her birthday. But I will be off for a couple of days afterwards. So I will make it up her. So far I really like her. She is not like any other girl I have been with. She has a real nice attitude about her. We decide to go to a little restaurant for lunch before I go to work. I give her the card and the bear. She likes both a lot.

"I have to go to work now" I tell her

"Ok be safe stop by and see me at my house" she tells me.

I drop her off at her house. Then I head to the station. It is only a couple of minutes away.

We start seeing more of each other. It is different we both tell each other we are just going to be friends. Nothing serious because we both just got out of bad relationships. When I am not around her, I miss her a lot. And this is unusual for me. One thing leads to another. We start doing things together. We decide to go to Manhattan to see the Christmas tree a Rockefeller Center. We notice that we enjoy being around each other.

"I am working a double on Christmas Day" I tell her.

"Ok well stop by and see me at my house" she replies.

"Ok I will" I respond.

Nothing happens Christmas Day. I stop by and see Irene. It is eleven at night. I am tired. I stop by see her and then head home to get some sleep. All the way home I am thinking of her.

Well the holidays have come and gone. It is a New Year and Irene and I are seeing each other on a regular basis. Each day we get closer and closer together. We finally decide to start seeing each other in a regular basis. I am very happy with decision.

THE LOST BATTALION

I report to the station as ordered. Irene and I have now been seeing each other for three months. She has moved in with me, we are both very happy.

"Hi Jimmy I heard you were assigned over here. What did you do over at the Four Nine Battalion"? Asks Lieutenant Cape.

"I got into an argument with Ken Bash. He blew it way out of proportion. It is a bunch of bull. You know what I mean. They called me on the phone and told me to report here. Who is the captain here?" I reply.

I have known Lieutenant Cape since I came to the field. He is a good and fair lieutenant. I am glad that I will be working with him know.

"It is captain Stein he very fair but he is by the book" Lieutenant Cape replies.

"Ok"

"You are going to be on Tour One for the first couple of weeks. Then you will be going to Tour Three. You will remain on A Platoon" he tells me.

In comes Captain Stein. He says hello and enters in office.

"I would like to see you in my office Mr. Thompson" he calls out to me.

I go in the office. I am wondering what is going on.

"All I want to do is go over the rules and regulations of the battalion with you. You must have your request in for leave by the fifteenth of the prior month. If not it will not be approved. There is no mutual policy at the station" he states to me.

He gives me a copy of the rules and regulations. I read through them and sign a copy for him. It looks like I will not be doing mutuals for a while. This will be rough. But other then that there are no major changes.

I report to Tour One. Go in the locker room put my uniform on and grab my gear. And go into the lieutenant's office.

"You are working with Allen McGuins. He is new and has only been you of the academy a couple of weeks. I am your lieutenant on Tour One." He tells me.

"Ok no problem" I reply.

I grab my gear and head toward the unit. Allen tells me it is a quite part of Queens. Not much goes on at nighttime where we are assigned.

We head out to our area. We decide to pull into this food store parking lot. There we are going to kick back and relax. All the sudden Allen yells.

"Lock your door. That is some guy trying to break into the bus"

Sure enough there is a guy outside trying to break into the bus. He looks like he is wasted on something. He is climbing all over the vehicle. Pulling on doors and pounding on the side with his fist.

"Queens Four-Five-Boy we need police at Grand and Fresh Street. There is a guy trying to break into the bus" I tell the dispatcher.

"Repeat Four-Five-Boy"

"There is a nut trying to break into the bus" I tell her.

"Ok sending police and a patrol boss to your location" she replies.

This guy is really high on something. He is really trying to get in. he is climbing all over the vehicle. So we can not drive away. He is wearing these green and white stripe jeans and an orange shirt. There is definitely a screw loose or something up stairs. It has been a couple of minutes now. You can hear the police car siren getting closer. The guy hears it to and starts running down the street. Allen and are sitting in the ambulance looking at each other. Like where did this nut come from. The police arrive and start taking down all the information for the report. Also Lieutenant Rock arrives on the scene and starts taking down all the information for his report. He tells us to write a statement of what happen. We finish all the paperwork. The rest of the night is slow and uneventful.

I have been on Tour One now for three weeks. I am told that staring next week I will be on Tour three preeminently. My new partners will be Bob Pale and Tom Long. We will work a new unit called Four-Five David. And we will sit down the street from Four-Five-Boy. We will be covering basically the same area. It will be different working in the afternoon. I will be home at nighttime sleeping in my own bed. I know Irene will be happy about this.

I report to work the next week on Tour Three. There is Lieutenant Cape in the office.

"I will be your lieutenant now" he tells me.

It is my first shift with Bob. He is new and came out of the same class as Allen. We head over to our area. It is not a bad area. There are no projects to respond to. That is one good thing. There is a high school there where we can kick back and relax.

All the sudden the radio calls out "Four-Five David for the assignment. You have a body recovery behind Fifty five Fifty Ninth Street"

It is dark out when we get the call. We start out for the assignment.

It is an easy job. Pick up the body and take it to the morgue. Just make sure all the paperwork is in order or they will not accept the body. Also make sure that the police ride in back with the body. We are driving pass a cemetery when I see something on the fence.

"Hey look at the fence there is a guy on the fence" I tell Bob.

Bob backs up the ambulance. And there is an older man up on the fence stuck.

"Hey what are you doing up on the fence" I call to him.

"I am stuck can you help me down" he replies.

We pull the ambulance up to the fence. We start to help him get down. He is not injured. About that time a police car arrives on the scene. We can him off the fence.

"I was at my wife's grave and they locked the gates on me. I tried to climb over the fence and got stuck" he tells us.

The police are taking down all the information. He thanks us and we head on to the body recovery. It is dark out and hard to find where the building is. We have driven up and down the street three times. When we finally find the location. It is a large abandon warehouse. We pull around the side of the building and see a police car. We also can hear the officers talking. We follow the voices to the back of the building. There we finally find the officers.

"Hey this is a hard a place to find" I tell them.

"Yea it is back in no mans land" officer replies.

"Where is the body"?

"Over hear! He fell off the roof. He was up on the roof drinking and fell off" the police tell us.

"Ok, does he have a ninety-five tag on him"?

"Yes it is on his right toe" the officer replies.

"Ok got it, let me fill out the paperwork. We will take him to the Queens Morgue. You know a police offer has to ride with him. Or they will not accept him at the morgue."

"Ok Officer Smith will ride with him" the officer states.

I get all the information. It takes me about fifteen minutes to fill out the paperwork. Bob is like let's get this over with. He does not like being around dead bodies. We go get the stretcher and a body bag. The guy is tall and thin. So it is a little hard to put him in the bag. At least he is not heavy or blotted. We finally get him in the bag and place the bag on the stretcher. We wheel him back to the bus. Load him in and take off for the morgue. It will take about thirty minutes to get there. This is an easy job as long as all the paperwork is in order. We arrive at the morgue in about twenty-five minutes there is a guy there to meet us.

"What do you guys have? He ask

"The guy from Fifty-Ninth Street that fell off the roof I reply.

He takes all the paperwork and starts going through it. If it is not correct he will not accept the body. Then it is a major hassle. You're stuck with a dead body in the back of your bus for a while.

"Ok I will accept the body. Just put it over there on the table". He tells us.

We place the body on the table. Bob is glad this job is over. We leave the morgue and start heading back to our area. We will back in are area in about fifteen minutes. The rest of the shift is quite and we head back to the battalion and go home.

It is starting to get cool out. Fall is not far away. Irene and I have been together six months now. Things are going good for us. We hung out on the beach all summer. I have been assigned to the Four-Five Battalion for six months. I like working with the people there. They are a good group to work with.

"Four-Five-David for the assignment. You have a violent emotionally disturbed person throwing furniture out the window at Fifty-Ten Grand Ave. PD and ESU have been assigned." The dispatcher tells us.

I hit the sixty-three button. Bob is copying down all the information on the report. We take off for the job. We head down Metropolitan to Flushing turn right. Head over to Grand Ave. As we head down Grand Ave. We see a chair come out the second floor window and hit the street. There is other furniture in the street also.

"Well I guess this guy is mad about something," I say

"Yea we will let the cops talk to him and restrain him" Bob replies.

There are three police cars on the scene.

"Hey guys this guy is on something. We went up to the apartment. But we can not get in. we called for ESU they have a ten-minute arrival time. Also we have a report that he has someone in the apartment with him" the officer tells us.

"So is the guy a barricaded in the apartment"? I ask.

"Yes he is" the officer replies.

"Ok I will call for a patrol boss" I tell Bob

We will be here all night.

"Four-Five-David to Citywide"

"Citywide Go ahead Four-Five-David"

"Four-Five-David can we have a patrol boss and a second unit. We have a barricaded EDP with a hostage at the scene"

"Ten-four will send you Conditions Four-Five" the dispatcher tells us.

Condition Four-Five arrives on the scene. It is Lieutenant Cape.

"What do you guys have"? He asks.

We advise him of the situation. He tells Citywide to send a second unit. He then gives them update report. He will be the officer in charge for the job.

We can hear ESU responding in the distance. ESU stands for the Emergency Service Unit. They are part of the police department. They handle all types of special emergencies. They patrol the city in large and small rescue trucks. They carry all types of special equipment in them. There are eleven of them in the city.

They have three smaller trucks that work with one large truck. ESU has arrived on the scene. There is one large truck here and three small trucks.

We now have the street blocked with all sorts of emergency equipment. It is starting to get dark now. We have been on the scene for at least an hour. The guy is still in the apartment. He does not want to talk to anyone. They have called for a hostage negotiator. He should be arriving soon.

He arrives and the patient still will not talk. We have now been on the scene for three hours. The police finally decide that they are going to use the tazer to take the guy down. The tazer shoots two wires into the patient. Then it charges the wires with electricity. And the patient passes out from the electrical charge. They call us over for meeting. The police give the patient one more chance. He refuses to talk. We start getting into position to take the door and subdue the patient.

We head up the stairs with our equipment. We are behind the police. They take the battering ram and hit the door three times. Each time you hear a loud bang. Finally the door gives away. It flies off the hinges and hits the floor. There is a big guy standing in the middle of room nude. He turns around, looks at us and starts charging towards us. The police lieutenant pulls out the tazer gun and shoots at the patient. You hear the pop of the tazer. Then you hear the loud crashing sound of the patient hitting the floor. The patient is knocked out and on the floor. We grab a sheet to cover him up. This guy is like seven feet tall and weighs about three hundred and fifty pounds. He looks like he works out.

We decide do to the size of the patient. We should secure him in the stokes basket. To take him down to the ambulance. The police now have this guy cuffed with his hands behind him. He still on the floor passed out. Two officers leave to get the basket from there truck. The police are searching the rest of the apartment. They find that he was in the apartment by himself. There is only one patient.

The officers arrive back in the apartment with the stokes basket. This guy is big and we roll him into the basket. They make sure he is secure. They have put these heavy straps across his legs. We are now securing him to the basket. He has not started to wake up yet. Now comes the fun part, trying to get him down the stairs and into the ambulance. It is decided to slide him down the hallway. Then let it slide down the stairs with us guiding it. I want to get him in the bus as soon as possible. I do not want this guy to wake up while we are moving him. Everything goes as planned. We get him in the bus. There are four police officers and Bob in back of the ambulance. One ESU truck is going to follow us to the hospital.

We have to take him to Elmhurst Hospital. It will take us about ten minutes to get there. I take off for the hospital. I can hear some yelling in the back. The patient is starting to wake up. He is yelling at the police. They tell to get to the hospital as fast as I can. I decide to call in a notification to the hospital.

"Four-Five-David to Citywide with a notification"

"Go ahead Four-Five-David" the dispatcher responds.

"Four-Five-David we are inbound hospital forty-six. We have a thirty-six year old male, no vitals available. The patient is restrained by ESU. Are ETA is about ten minutes. Please have hospital police standing by"

"Ten-four hospital notified"

We arrive at the hospital in about ten minutes. There are other units there that can help us. We pull the stretcher out and head into the emergency room. There is a doctor and a nurse waiting for us as we enter the hospital.

They direct us to a small room on the left. Bob gives the doctor a report. He decides to leave the patient secured to the stretcher. He then orders a shot to knock the patient out. The patient is screaming and trying to spit at everybody. But his faced is covered with a sheet. Bob gets the report signed. They give the guy the shot. He passes out in a couple of minutes. We then roll the guy onto their stretcher. He is now their problem. Are shift is about over. We head back to the station.

It is wintertime and cold out. Irene and I are talking about all sorts of things. I really like her and have decided to pop the question. We head out to the beach at three-forty in the mourning on March seventh. The wind is blowing and the sand is frozen solid. It is freezing out as we walk to the beach. We are about three hundred feet from the house. As we walk we are talking about various things. We have talked about marriage a couple of times. We get to the beach walk out on the sand. I kneel down on one knee and ask her.

"Would you marry me"?

"Are you serious"? She replies.

"Yes I am"

"Ok yes I will"

I place the ring on her finger. We are both very excited as we head back to the house.

We have decided to get married on the date we meant. That will be December twelve. I am looking forward to it. She is starting to make all the plans. I never new there was so much planning to get married. We decided to get married in my fire department dress uniform. The two friends I have asked are on the job. They will wear their dress uniform to. I am working a lot of overtime to pay for the wedding. She is working and saving money to for the wedding. She went with her cousin today to pick out the wedding dress. Spring will be here soon. And it will be warm out again.

We decide to go down the street for a soda. All the sudden we hear all these sirens. There are police cars all over the intersection where we are assigned. We hear the dispatcher call Four-Five-Boy for a shooting down the street from where we are.

"Four-Five-David that is our job we will pick it up, we are on the scene" I tell the dispatcher.

We stop in front of a barbershop. A police officer signals us to come in to shop. I grab my gear and head into the shop.

Inside I find a guy lying in the back of the shop. He has been shot in the head. You can see brain matter leaking from the wound. I grab a dressing and start applying slight pressure. Bob is grabbing a board, collar and the stretcher.

"Is he likely"? The cop asks.

I nod my head yes. I can hear more sirens in the background. I hope one of them is a medic unit. Bob enters the shop with all the equipment. We start packaging the patient for transport. We get him secured and head to the bus. As we are getting ready to load him the medics arrive on scene.

I am glad to see them. They are a fire department medic unit.

"Where is he shot"? The medic asks.

"In the side of his head, No exit wound" I reply.

His breathing is getting louder. You can see him gasping for air. I am bagging him with a bag valve mask. The medic is getting ready to tube him. This is a tube that they put down his throat into his lungs. It gives you a sealed airway. The medic tells us to move. He gets the tube in on the first try. I then hook the mask to the tube and squeeze the bag. This forces oxygen into the lungs. You can see the chest rise with each squeeze of the bag. The patient is still hanging on to life. The medic tells Bob to head to the trauma center. His partner will call the hospital with the notification.

We take off for the trauma center. I am still bagging him. The medic is giving him various medications. The monitor shows he still has a pulse. But you can see that this guy is going to go into cardiac arrest soon. We are heading down Elliot Street to Queens Boulevard. We turn left onto Queens Boulevard and head to Broadway. Where we turn right and head to the hospital. As we pull into the hospital the patient goes into cardiac arrest. We take him into the trauma room. The trauma team starts working on him. But he does not make it.

Bob has gone outside to start cleaning up the back of the ambulance. We will have to go back to the station. I have blood and matter on my uniform. I have to shower and change my uniform. We will at the station for a while cleaning up everything. I am getting done cleaning up and putting a clean uniform on when the police stop by.

"Where you guys on the shooting"? The cops ask

"Yes" I reply.

"He was shot by the barber two doors down. The barber was mad that this guy was taking his customers" the cop tells us.

I think to myself only in New York can you get shoot for that. The end of the shift is fast approaching. I will be off for the next three days. I am shore that Irene has something planned. Or we will be on the beach hanging out.

"Four-Five-David for the burn major" the radio calls out.

"Four-Five-David give it up"

"Four-Five-David respond to Six-Nine Street and Fresh Ponds Road for the burn major. You have a three-year-old boy with burns to the head. Be advised you have medics responding" the dispatcher tells us.

"Four-Five-David ten-four responding"

We head down Metropolitan to Fresh Ponds turn right go five blocks and we are on the scene. We get there in about two minutes.

There is a baby in his mother's arm yelling in pain. He has second degree burns to his head from hot water. I take a dressing and soak it in cool water. Then I place it on the burned area. I tell Tom we have to go to the burn center in Manhattan. He agrees and gets ready to make the notification. The medics have not arrived yet. We cancel them and get ready to head to the hospital. It will take us at least thirty minutes to get there.

Tom starts heading down Metropolitan Avenue to Elliot to Queens Boulevard. Then down Queens Boulevard and over the Fifty-Ninth Street Bridge and in to Manhattan. He turns right on First Street and heads north to Seventy-Seventh Street. The hospital is on the right side of the street. We get there in about twenty minutes. I feel sorry for all the pain the little boy is in. I hope the burns do not scar him for life. We take the patient into the emergency room. They take the child from us and enter the burn unit. You are not allowed to enter the burn unit. I would like to go and see how they treat burn victims sometime.

It is getting closer to the wedding. Irene is making all the plans. I am staying out of the way. We are going to look at the church today. It is an old church located in Corona Queens. I am responsible for writing the directions to the church. So everybody can get there. She is taking care of all the arrangements. We are also making the final arrangements for the honeymoon.

It was a nice couple of days off. Now it is time to get back to work. I head to the station thinking about the wedding and everything else. I am a little nerve. But I am working with Tom tonight. So it will be a fun shift. I put my equipment on the ambulance and do a check out sheet. I am driving since it is my first night back. All the sudden the radio calls out.

"Four-Five-David for the EDP"

"Four-Five-David give it up"

"Four-Five-David respond to the female EDP at sixty-six Street and Cooper on the second floor"

It is not far from where we are. We get there in a couple of minutes. There is a lot of yelling on the second floor. We head up the stairs. There are a couple of firefighters in the room. They have the lady flat on the floor. She is screaming and trying to get loose. We bring the chair in to the room to secure her to it.

"What do you guys have"? Tom asks

"She smoked some crack and now wants to kill everybody" the captain replies.

It takes all of us to secure her the stair chair. All the sudden BAM she kicks me in the jaw. I go flying back into a chest of draws. I can not even move my jaw. It hurts real bad and is swollen.

The firefighters grab and restrain her. The captain calls for a second unit. I think I have a fractured jaw. My mouth is swelling up and I can not talk. All I can do is make sounds. There are a couple of units responding now. They heard Tom put out the call for help and injured member of service. Two units arrive on the scene. The police are their now. They are placing her under arrest. Four-Nine-

Boy is going to take me to the hospital. My jaw is feeling a little better now. We get to the hospital in a couple minutes.

They take me in right away. I can move my jaw some but it still hurts. The doctor orders the x-rays and does his examination. After about an hour they release me. I only have a sever bruise. Thank goodness I only have a month to the wedding. How would it look if I could not talk at the wedding? I will be off for a week. I can use that time to get ready for the big day.

The big day finely arrives. I get to the church around one in the afternoon. Our wedding is at two. It is a nice day outside. Yes I am nervous as I walk into the church. I am wearing my fire department dress uniform. It is a tradition in my family to get married in your dress uniform. Everybody else is at the church. It is getting close to the time. Frank is there he is my best man.

"Hey Frank do you see Irene"? I ask.

"No the limo just arrived" he replies

"She should be in it"

"She is not"

"Are you sure"?

"Yea, the limo driver forgot to pick her up" Frank tells me.

By now I am walking up and down the hallway in the back of the church. The limo driver leaves to go get her and he gets lost. He shows back up at the church thirty minutes late with her.

She looks gorgeous as she walks down the isle of the church. The wedding goes off without any other problems. In twenty minutes I am now married to Irene Thompson. We head over to the reception. From there it is off on the honeymoon.

It is January now. I have been married for a whole month. I am at work when the phone rings.

"Hey Cali you got a call, it's the wife" Lieutenant Cape tells me.

"Hello"

"Jim, are you sitting down"? Irene asks.

"No should I"I reply.

"I think you better, I just took two pregnancy test and they are positive" she replies.

"WHAT ARE YOU SURE" I yell into the phone.

"Yes it is positive I am pregnant"

"Take a third while I am on the phone"

"Yes it is positive I am pregnant"

"Holy crap I am going to be a daddy"I yell.

I tell everybody in the station. They all start telling me congratulations.

"Hey Cali you have transfer orders here. You are being transferred to Lower Manhattan Battalion Four. You are going to be assigned to Zero-Four-Henry. You can not stay hear they do not have a Haz-Tec assigned here. It has been fun working with you" Lieutenant Cape tells me.

"It was fun working with you to sir" I reply.

TIME IN MANHATTAN

I have been transferred to Lower Manhattan Battalion Four. They say Lower Manhattan is the place to be assigned. That there are a lot of good looking women all over the place. And you get a lot of unusual jobs here. I called the station on my day off and talked to the scheduling officer. He told me I would be working Tour One and to report on Sunday night.

I leave my house around twenty-two hundred hours. This gives me about an hour to get to work. I will take the Van Wyck Expressway to the Long Island Expressway to the Brooklyn-Queens Expressway to the Williamsburg Bridge and into Lower Manhattan. While I am driving I am thinking about the station. Will I like it there? Will I have good partners? This is all going through my mind as I drive. I get into Lower Manhattan according to the map. I take Allen Street to the station. The station is next to the river. I drive along the river and finally find the station. It is not hard to get to. It is not that bad of a drive to work.

I park my truck and head into the station.

"Hi my name is James Thompson, I was told to report Tour One on Zero-Four-Henry by Lieutenant Lewis" I tell the desk lieutenant.

"I am Lieutenant Lewis, Welcome to the station. The locker room is on the third floor. Go find a locker put your name and shield on it. Then come back down I have some paperwork for you fill out." he replies.

I go upstairs find a locker and put my gear in it. Then I put my name and shield on it. Then I go back downstairs see the lieutenant and fill out the paperwork. The station seams pretty nice.

"Hey Thompson do you want to work Zero-One-Charlie tonight since you are extra"? The lieutenant ask me.

"Sure where does it sit"?

"Thompson and Grand Street in the West Village. You will be working with Betty Ace"? He replies.

"Hi I am Betty are you working with me? I do not like to drive". She tells me.

We head out to the ambulance. She does the check out sheet. I log us on to the computer.

"First can we stop by Starbucks please"? She asks.

Betty is very polite and fun to work with. We are in our area. There are a lot of strange people in the village. People where all sorts of clothes and dress really different. All the sudden the radio calls out.

"Zero-One-Charlie for the assignment. You have an injury at the corner of Bleaker and Jones. This is an interesting call be safe" she tells us.

The call comes over the computer screen. I am reading the call. It states that there is a twenty-five year old male on the corner with a swollen penis. This should be interesting. We start heading toward the call. I am reading the map. I do not now the area that well yet. It is my first shift in Lower Manhattan. Betty does not now it real well. She has only been in the field a couple of weeks. We get there in a couple of minutes.

There is a guy standing on the corner waving at us. We pull up to him.

"Did you call for an ambulance"? I ask him

"Yea my dick is swollen and it hurts. I want to go to Saint Vincent's Hospital". He replies.

"Do you want me to get in the back with this guy"? I ask Betty

"No I got it. Just give me a couple minutes to do the paperwork". She replies.

We are on the scene for about ten minutes.

"Ok we can go now" she tells me.

I start out for the hospital. It is only a couple of blocks away. I looked it up on the map while she was getting the information. We get there in about three minutes.

Betty comes out of the emergency room.

"That was an interesting job" I say.

"Yes this is an interesting area of the city to work" she replies.

They say you can get to the point that nothing surprises you any more in New York City and they are right. I like working Tour One especially in Lower Manhattan. All the strange people are out running around. It makes for an interesting shift.

"Four-Zero-Henry for the assignment, you have a labor at 1226 Avenue A" the dispatcher tells us.

"Ten-four send it over" I reply.

Greg is tech and I am the driver. I start heading to the call. We head down Houston Street to Avenue A and turn right. It is about one in the mourning so there is no traffic. We get there in about five minutes.

"Come in" a lady says.

We enter the apartment and find a lady nine months pregnant on the couch. Greg starts asking her all the standard questions. She is giving him the information. I am filling out the Ambulance Call Report. We put her in the stair chair and wheel her out to the ambulance. Her pains are about two minutes apart. Bellevue Hospital is about four minutes away. I hit the eighty-two button and type in hospital zero two. That is the code for Bellevue.

I head over Fourteenth Street to the Franklin D. Roosevelt Drive and head north. The hospital is two exits up at Thirty-Fifth Street. We get off on Thirty-

Fifth Street and head toward the emergency room entrance. I back the ambulance up to the entrance and go get a hospital stretcher. I open the doors to the back of the ambulance. There is Greg getting ready to deliver the baby. The baby's head is already coming out. We deliver the baby in the back of the ambulance. Then place mom and baby on the hospital stretcher and head into the emergency room. Mom and son are doing fine.

It is about seven in the mourning close to tour change. All the sudden the radio comes to life.

"Zero-Four-Henry for the assignment. You have a stabbing at Twelve-twelve Columbia Street apartment Fifty-two A. On the fifth floor. Police are on the location" the dispatcher tells us.

I turn on the siren and lights and hit the responding button. It is just around the corner from where we are. We head down Houston and turn left on Columbia Street. The address is half way down the street on the left. It is easy to find there are four police cars out front. So it is safe to go to the apartment.

We head over to the elevators. All the sudden the doors open. Here comes a male with a wound to his left arm. He has scratches all over his chest and arms.

"What happen"? Ask Greg.

"My girlfriend cut me because I called out this other girls name while I was sleeping. She got pissed off and cut me". He replied.

This sounds interesting. We place him in the back of the bus. Greg starts treating him. I am outside getting all the information from the cops. Then they bring the girlfriend out. She is under arrest. She is yelling at them that they cannot arrest her. This is because she has a child and is on welfare. The cops are not really listening to her. They put her in the police car. Greg has finished up treating the patient. We will take him to Bellevue Hospital. This will be are last job for the shift. It has been an interesting night in Lower Manhattan.

It is now summer time in the city. There are good looking women all over the place. There is nothing like working in Lower Manhattan. I am working overtime today with Bob Fine. We are working ambulance Zero-One-Boy. It is assigned downtown at Church and Liberty Streets. It has been a quite mourning. When all the sudden we get a call for an abdominal pain in one of the office towers.

Bob is driving and we get there in a couple of minutes. We have to walk down the street to the office building. It is one of the high-rise buildings. We get there and security is holding the elevator for us. We got up to the fifty-fifth floor. There we enter a large office area. A girl meets us and tells us to follow her to the conference room. We enter the room. There is catered food all over the table. It really looks good. A lot better then what we eat while at work. The patient is sitting in a chair.

"Hello I am Bob from the Fire Department Emergency Medical Service may we help you"? Bob ask.

"I think it is gas. I do not want to go to hospital. I wish they did not call you. I am fine really" she replies.

We tell her about are protocols. She then explains to us that she does not want to go to hospital. I then explain the refuse medical aid form that has to be filled out. She tells us she will sign the back of the report.

"Hey you guys take a plate and get some food it's free" a lady tells us.

We are like alright. This food looks good. We will not have to buy lunch today. We each take a plate and put some food on it.

"No you guys can eat more then that. Here take this with you I insist" she responds.

She hands us each a plate piled high with food. We thank her take the food and leave the office.

We head out to the elevator and take it down to the lobby. We head out in to the nice summer day. Back in the bus we finish up the paperwork. Then we start eating all the food. It is good and I am stuffed and feel like taking a nap. We head back to our area. Still we are talking about all the food we were given. It is getting close to tour change. We start heading back to the battalion. It has been a nice day in Lower Manhattan. I am still full as I drive home from the station. The one thing I notice is during the day. You can always tell who the tourists are. They take pictures of everything. Some will even stand up in the tour bus and take pictures of us responding to jobs. I think to myself there are better things to take pictures of then fire department vehicles. I think to myself I could handle working days here. But then you have to deal with traffic and chiefs always checking up on you. No I will stay on Tour One. It takes me a little over an hour to get home due to all the traffic.

It is about ten at night. I am getting ready to go to work. Irene is relaxing she is now seven months pregnant. So it is a little hard to get around. I head into the city drinking a Diet Coke. I am thinking about my son that will be here soon. I arrive at the station in about an hour. I will kick back downstairs with the other crews waiting for my unit to get back. Mr. Happy and Mr. Miserable are working together tonight. They complain about everything. They could win a million dollars. And they would still be mad about something.

They finally arrive at the station. I put my gear on the unit. Greg is coming out to log on to the computer. I hope it will be a quite night. I did not get much sleep in the afternoon. We log on and head out for Greg's coffee. Greg has to have his coffee. He is a lot fun to work with. He is very calm and never gets excited about anything. I am just starting to get comfortable when the dispatcher calls us. We have to respond to a hazardous materials job in mid town Manhattan. It is at West Forty-Seventh Street and Seventh Avenue.

We start heading up to the job. There is a lot of radio traffic on the Citywide in reference to the call. We arrive in about fifteen minutes. There is already a hazmat boss there. We are told we have to suit up. We will be using the yellow splash suits with air. That there was steam pipe explosion and that there is asbestos contamination. We will be at this job all night. It is a hot and humid night. So it will be rough working in the suits. Suit time could be as little as ten minutes.

We start putting on the suits. They are bulking and we are sweating. We have are air packs on. But have not been told to go on air yet. They take us over to the merv. This is a large mobile emergency room. You can perform surgery in it. There are five of these in the city. They have the air conditioning set real cold. It feels real good with the suits on. Finally the deacon trailer arrives. They are setting it up for operation.

I am feeling a little sick now. But decide that I am alright and still can do my job. I leave the merv and head toward the trailer. We are now going on air. That means the suits are getting sealed up. And that we will be breathing air through mask from are air packs. I feel a little worse now. I did not have much water to drink before the call. All the sudden the next thing I know I feel real dizzy. Then all the sudden there is John Witter.

"What happen you need to go to hospital. You are dehydrated". He tells me.

They have already cut my suit off me. They have cut most of my uniform off. The other paramedic is starting two intravenous lines in me. She is putting one in each arm. I am in the merv. I do not now how I got there.

"You passed out. You were down for a good ten minutes". She tells me.

I am starting to get my senses back. I know understand what is going on around me.

"We are taking you to Bellevue Hospital" she tells me.

"Ok but do not let a voluntary hospital unit transport me" I yell.

"We know better then that. We are going to take you" she replies.

In the city there are ambulances that are operated by private hospital. They are called voluntary units. They are manned by personal not trained to fire department standards. And the last thing I want is one of these units touching me. They load me in to back of the ambulance and start out for the hospital. We will be there in a couple of minutes. We get there they take me into the emergency room. I know some of the nurses and they are taking good care of me. I have gotten some fluid back in me. I am starting to feel better know.

I have been in the hospital for a couple of hours. The doctor comes in the room.

"We can discharge you know. All I want to do is check your temperature before you leave". He tells me

The nurse comes in and checks my temperature. It is normal.

"Ok it is normal you are discharged. Good luck and be safe" he tells me.

I sign out of the hospital. Greg is waiting for me outside. I climb in the ambulance.

"Well this tour is over. How do you feel"? He ask

"I feel pretty good, a little weak still. All I want to do is go home and get some sleep". I reply.

We head back to the station. We will be there in about ten minutes. Then I have a lot of paperwork to fill out. There is like ten different forms you have to fill out. That will take about an hour to do. At least I will be on overtime. So they will rush to get the paperwork done.

I finally get all the paperwork done. Head up to my locker change and get ready to head home. It will take an extra half hour this mourning. This is due to all the traffic on the expressways. So I stop at McDonalds on the way home for some breakfast.

Irene is really starting to feel the baby kick. We are getting close to the due date. It will be any time in the next couple of weeks. I will be a daddy for the first time. I am very nervous about that. I think about it all the time when I am driving to from work. I get to the station a little early. Nothing has happen in the days I was off. Greg shows up and we take off for coffee.

"Four-Zero-Henry for the assignment. You have a stabbing at Twenty-four, Twenty Station Street. Police are on the scene." the dispatchers tells us.

"Ten-four put it on the screen" I reply.

The job appears on the computer. It is a small street off of Columbia. All we have to do is go down Houston Street. Turn right on to Columbia and turn on to Station. We get there in about two minutes. Two guys come running up to the unit. One guy is holding a towel over his forehead. The towel is soaked with blood.

He is yelling "I got cut in the head".

As he is climbing into the back of the bus, he is bleeding from the temple and the blood is spurting out with force. So I now that an artery has been cut. I start apply pressure to the wound. He has collapsed on the stretcher.

"Hey Greg lets get rolling to Bellevue. This guy has a lacerated Temple artery. Give them a note twenty year old male, no vitals". I yell to Greg.

Greg takes off for the hospital. There blood all over me and the back of the ambulance. I am holding pressure on the wound. I also have to get him on oxygen and check for other injuries. It seams like it is taking longer then usual to get there. We get to the hospital in three minutes. Greg was hauling ass up the FDR Drive.

We back up to the emergency room. There is another crew there to help us. We unload the stretcher. The trauma team is there waiting for the patient as we rush into the trauma room. The doctor is calling out orders. He then asks us.

"What happen"? The doctor ask

"Twenty year old male. Laceration to forehead and the temple artery, Unable to control bleeding, no vitals available" I reply.

I leave the room and start writing up the report. There is blood all over me and the back of the ambulance. We will be out of service while we clean everything up. I am asking his friend as much information as possible. He is giving me what he can. It takes about thirty minutes to finish the report. I go in and get the signature from nurse. They are getting the patient ready for surgery. We get ready to head back to the station.

We get to the station. Greg starts cleaning the back of the ambulance. I go upstairs and take a shower. Put on a clean uniform. Then I try and find a way to clean my boots. They have blood all over them.

"Hey Cali you can not work with those boots on. You are going to have to get them replaced. I am placing you guys off service" Lieutenant Lewis tells us.

We only have a couple of hours left on the shift. I will have to go to quartermaster tomorrow and get a new pair.

I go and get my new boots. Irene and her friend are in the car. She is telling me that I should carry my driver's license with me all the time. Because I have a bad habit of leaving it at work. So we decided to go to the station and drop off the boots and pick up my license. First we stop by the house. We are heading down the Van Wyck Expressway.

Irene yells"Jim I think I am in labor"

"How far apart are the pains"?

"They are about six minutes apart" she replies.

"Ok that is not active labor" I reply.

We get on the Brooklyn Queens Expressway.

"The pains are getting closer" she yells.

"How far are they now"? I ask

"They are about two minutes apart" she replies.

I think to myself holly shit an explosive birth. I see a highway patrol officer in his car. I show him my shield and explain the problem. I tell him I need to get to my station on South Street. He tells me to follow him over the bridge to the station. I call my station on the cell phone.

"Hello Lieutenant this is Cali. I am in bound with Irene she is going to have the baby. It looks like there might be complications. Please have a bus standing by. I should be there in about five minutes".

"Got it" he replies.

We roll into the station. There are emergence lights all over the place. There is basic life support unit, advance life support unit, patrol boss, and two police cars at the station. We place her in the back of the ambulance. I am so nervous that I can hardly give any information on her. We will take her to Downtown Hospital. We take off for the hospital. Everybody is going sirens and lights. We get to the hospital in a couple of minutes. We back up to the emergency room entrance. There are other units there.

"Hey Cali what's going on"? somebody ask

"Irene is having the baby" I reply.

"Ok I got the elevator" somebody yells.

We head through the emergency room to the waiting elevator. I am nervous as all get out. Irene is yelling in labor pains. We get into the delivery are and enter the room assigned to us by the nurse. The doctor comes in and starts examining Irene. He orders a sonogram.

After he reads the sonogram, he enters the room to talk to us.

"Everything looks good, but she is not going to deliver tonight. But it will be in the next forty-eight hours" he tells us.

I am still sweating. Irene is starting to relax and telling me to. We head back down to the emergency room. If there is a unit there we get a ride back to the station. At the station we pick up the car and my license. Drop her friend off and head home.

I am getting ready to go to work. Irene and her sister are at the house.

"Love you, is everything ok"? As I leave the house.

All the way to work I am thinking about her going to in to labor. I get to the station a little early. Lieutenant Lewis is there. We talk a little about last night. I tell him what the doctor told me. Greg comes in and we getting ready to go to work. Greg signs us on to the computer. I check out the unit. It is a quite night.

All the sudden we are told of a hazardous materials assignment in Central Manhattan. We start heading to the job.

We are half way there when all the sudden my beeper starts going off with my number and nine one one after it. I call the house.

"What's up"? I ask

"I am in labor its for real this time Jim get home" Irene replies.

"Ok call the station and tell them. We are responding to a job". I tell her.

A couple of minutes later it comes over the computer that we are out of service. We head back to the station. I jump out of the truck and put my gear away and change out of my uniform. I then take off out of the station.

I am in the car. I look down and see that I am in going ninety miles an hour. It is two in the mourning and there is no traffic on the road. I see a gas station off to the right. I pull in and put ten dollars of gas in. I get to the house in twenty-two minutes. That is a new record. Irene is already waiting for me as I enter the house.

"Let's go to the hospital" she yells in pain.

I help her out to the car. We take off for the hospital. It will take us fifteen minutes to get there.

I call the station and tell them what is going on. That this is real and not false labor. For the next twelve hours Irene is in labor with. Then finally at two in the afternoon she delivers our son Kevin. He delivers with out complications. I call the station and tell the desk lieutenant that my son was born and that I will be back in twelve weeks. I get to hold him for the first time. I am very nervous and proud. This is the first time I will be off for all three holidays.

"Zero-Four-Henry respond to a report of boat into a pier. The location is pier Forty-four on the Westside" the dispatcher tells us.

We start heading over the Westside. We will take Houston Street to the West-side Highway. There we go north to the pier. We arrive on the scene. And there sure enough, there is a large sightseeing boat into a building. There is emergency equipment all over the place. There are no injuries. All we are told to do standby. After about an hour we are released and head back to the station. I will be off for the next couple of days. And of course I will be home playing with my son.

It is a nice fall evening as I drive to the station. I am wondering what kind of night it will be. I hope it will be slow. But I know since it is warm out it will be busy. I arrive at the station just in time to get dressed and fall in for roll call. Lieutenant Chic has roll call and gives us information on up coming events. After roll call we head out to the truck and put our equipment on. As we put the equipment on the radio calls out.

"Zero-Four-Henry for the drug at Twelve twenty four West First Street" the dispatcher tells us.

"Zero-Four-Henry put it on the screen" I reply

We head over to the job. It is only five blocks from the station. We get there in a couple minutes. There is a female standing out front with a cowboy hat on.

"He is upstairs, he has been drinking and will not wake it up" she tells us.

I grab my bag and head up the stairs. There on the floor in the living room is a male with his pubic are packed in ice. There most be four inches of ice on top of his groin.

"Hey we tried to wake him up. He did not move so that is what you do to overdoses" she tells us.

I am thinking to myself this guy must be out of it. His balls are frozen and he is not moving. We get him up and put him in a chair. He is starting to wake up a little. But he can not give us any information. She gives us his information. I start filling out the report. This guy is only drunk. He must have been drinking heavily to be in this condition.

We run him over to the hospital and drop him off. We are done and back in service in about an hour. One good thing this guy did not vomit in the back of the bus. So at least we have no clean up to do. We are heading back to the station when the radio comes to life.

"Zero-Four-Henry switch to Citywide for the hazardous materials assignment in the Bronx. The location is One Three Six Street and Stann Ave." the dispatcher tells us.

"Zero-Four-Henry to Citywide responding" I reply

This about a thirty minute run for us. First we have to find where in the Bronx the job is. I do not now the Bronx at all. Greg finds it on the map. It close to the Third Avenue Bridge. So it will not be hard to get to. We get there in about thirty minutes. The computer tells us that there is a smell in the back of a garbage truck. The incident commander comes over and tells us.

"We are standing by. That someone through a battery in the garbage and it leaked. We should be able to take up in thirty minutes." he tells us

We finally get the order to take up. I am in a hurry to get back to Manhattan. We did not have to suit up. So it was an easy job. The rest of the night is quite.

Today is Election Day in the city. We are all hanging around in the station. When all the sudden all hell breaks loose.

"Hey you guys grab a reserve unit and head to the towers. There is major fire respond as Four-Seven-Mary. Lieutenant Arms tells us.

We put our equipment on the truck and head to the World Trade Center.

ABOUT THE AUTHOR

James H. Thompson

James Thompson started his career in emergency services when he was twelve. He became a member of Good Fellowship Ambulance Club in West Chester Pa. There he meant two important people in his life. They are Anthony Polito and Alan Levine. From there he entered the service where he became a combat medic. After the service he located to California where he became a career firefighter/ EMT till he was laid off in 1991. At that time he applied for New York City and was hired June of 1991. He was forced to retire in August 2004 from injuries he received on 9/11/2001.

978-0-595-37519-6
0-595-37519-7